Contents

Canna Apple Pecan Space Cake

Preparation Time: 20 minutes

Cooking Time: 45 minutes

Servings: 4-6

Ingredients:

- 1 cup flour
- 1/2 cup whole wheat flour
- 1/4 tsp. cinnamon
- 1/2 tsp. baking soda
- 1/2 tsp. nutmeg
- 1/2 tsp. salt
- 1 egg
- 1 cup granulated
- 2/3 cup canna oil
- 1/2 cup pecans chopped
- 2 apples, peeled and grated
- 1 gala apple, thinly sliced
- 15 pecan halves

For the glaze:

- 1/4 cup brown sugar
- 2 tsp. cannabis oil
- 2 tsp. water

Directions:

1. Heat your oven to 325 degrees Fahrenheit. Lightly coat a 9-inch spring form pan with nonstick cooking spray, In a medium bowl, combine the cinnamon, flours, baking soda, nutmeg and salt until blended. Whisk sugar and egg with the 2/3 cup cannabis-infused olive oil in a bowl. Stir the flour mixture into the egg mixture, and add the chopped pecans and grated apples. Scrape into the prepared pan and flatten the top of it, Arrange the apple slices on top of the edge of the cake, and arrange the pecan halves in one layer in the center.
2. Make the glaze in a small bowl. Mix together the brown sugar and the 2 tsp. olive oil and water and microwave in thirty-second intervals until the brown sugar is melted. Brush the apples and pecan with half of the glaze and save the rest.
3. Bake in the center of the oven until a toothpick when inserted in the middle of the cake comes out clean. Remove the pan out of the oven and brush the top of the warm cake with the rest of the glaze. Gently remove the cake from the base then serve.

Nutrition:

Calories: 290 Fat: 7.2g Fiber: 4.1 Carbs: 46g Protein: 3.4g

Canna Carrot Muffins

Preparation Time: 15 minutes

Cooking Time: 25-30 minutes

Servings: 10-12

Ingredients:

- 1¾ cups flour
- 1 teaspoon salt
- 1 teaspoon cinnamon
- 1teaspoon ground ginger
- ½ teaspoon grated nutmeg
- ¼ teaspoon baking soda
- ⅛ teaspoon baking powder
- 1 cup maple syrup
- ½ cup solid CBD Coconut Oil melted, or ¼ cup CBD Oil mixed with ¼ cup vegetable oil
- ½ cup milk
- 1 tablespoon fresh lemon juice
- 1 teaspoon vanilla extract
- 2 cups grated carrot
- ½ cup crushed pineapple, drained
- ½ cup each raisin, coconut, and pecans (or any nuts you like)

Directions:

1. Preheat the oven to 350°F. Line two 12-cup muffin tins with muffin papers or grease and flour the tins. In a large bowl, combine the flour, salt, cinnamon, ginger, nutmeg, baking soda, and baking powder. In a separate bowl, combine the maple syrup, coconut oil, milk, lemon juice, and vanilla. Combine both the wet and dry ingredients then fold it gently until just combined (over mixing makes the muffins tough). Fold in the carrots, pineapple, raisins, coconut, and pecans. Fill the prepared muffin tins two-thirds full. Let the cake bake for around 25 minutes or more or until a toothpick inserted into the center of a muffin comes out clean. Let them cool a little before serving.

Nutrition:

Calories: 200 Fat: 5.1g Fiber: 2tgg Carbs: 25.8g Protein: 1.2g

Rum Raisin Cupcakes

Preparation Time:

Cooking Time:

Servings:

Ingredients:

- Rum Raisins

- ¼ cup dark rum
- ½ cup golden raisins
- Cupcakes
- 1 cup all-purpose flour
- 1¼ teaspoons baking powder
- ¼ teaspoon ground cinnamon
- ⅛ teaspoon ground allspice
- ⅛ teaspoon freshly grated nutmeg
- ½ cup cannabutter, slightly softened
- 2 tablespoons unsalted butter, slightly softened
- ¾ cup firmly packed light brown sugar
- 3 large eggs
- 1 tablespoon pure vanilla extract
- ¼ teaspoon pure rum extract
- Sweet Cream Frosting
- ¼ cup unsalted butter, slightly softened
- ½ cup heavy cream
- 2 cups powdered sugar, sifted
- ⅛ teaspoon salt

Directions:

1. Prepare the rum raisins: In a small saucepan, warm the rum over low heat. Blend in the raisins and put it away from heat. Put the mix in a bowl, and then cover it with a saran wrap and let sit at room temperature for at least 6 hours or overnight. Prepare the cupcakes: Bring the temperature of your oven to 180c Put paper liners in the muffin tin. Ina medium bowl, stir together the flour, baking powder, cinnamon, allspice, and nutmeg. Set aside. Ina large bowl using an electric mixer, beat together the cannabutter, regular butter, and brown sugar on medium to high speed until you see that it becomes light and cloudlike, gradually add eggs, beating well after each addition. Beat in the vanilla and rum extracts. Reduce the speed mixer to low, add the flour mixture, and mix until just combined. Fold in the rum raisins and any remaining liquid. Scoop up the cupcake batter into the pan. Bake it for about 20 to 25 minutes, or until golden brown and a toothpick inserted into the center of a cupcake comes out clean. Let cool in the tin for 5 minutes, and then transfer to a wire rack to cool completely. Cupcakes without frosting can be stored up to 3 months. Prepare the sweet cream frosting: In a medium bowl using an electric mixer, beat the butter on medium speed until creamy. Lower down the speed to medium and add the cream and 1 cup of the powdered sugar; beat until well combined. Slowly add the remaining1 cup sugar and the salt. Put the frosting to a piping bag fitted with the tip of your choice and frost the cupcakes, or simply frost them with a butter knife or small offset spatula. Store the frosted cupcakes in an airtight container in the refrigerator for up to 1 week.

Nutrition:

Calories: 215 Fat: 5g Fiber: 4.1 Carbs: 35.6g Protein: 2g

Hot Ganja Chocolate Cupcakes

Preparation Time: 10 minutes

Cooking Time: 20-25 minutes

Servings: 2-4

Ingredients:

- ½ Cup all-purpose flour
- 1 tsp. Baking Powder
- Pinch Salt
- 1/3 Cup Cocoa
- ½-1 t Hot Red Pepper Flakes
- 2 tbsp. canna oil
- Scant ½ Cup of milk
- ½ tsp. Vanilla
- ¼ tsp. Apple Cider Vinegar
- ¼ Cup Sugar

Directions:

1. Preheat oven to 365°. Combine Flour, Baking Powder, Salt and Sugar. Whisk! Add wet ingredients and whisk until completely smooth. Fill 4-5 cupcake liners 2/3 full. Bake for 20 minutes or until a toothpick comes out clean. Allow to cool completely before frosting.

Nutrition:

Calories: 187 Fat: 4.3g Fiber: 2g Carbs: 29.6g Protein: 1g

French Toast Cupcakes

Preparation Time: 20 minutes

Cooking Time: 20-25 minutes

Servings: 12

Ingredients:

- Topping
- ¼ cup all-purpose flour
- ¼ cup of sugar
- 2½ tablespoons unsalted butter, cut into ½-inch pieces and chilled
- ½ teaspoon ground cinnamon
- ¼ cup chopped pecans
- Cupcakes
- 1½ cups all-purpose flour
- 1 cup of sugar
- 1½ teaspoons baking powder
- 1 teaspoon ground cinnamon
- ½ teaspoon ground allspice
- ¼ teaspoon freshly grated nutmeg

- ½ teaspoon salt
- ½ cup cannabutter slightly softened
- ½ cup sour cream
- 2 large eggs
- ½ teaspoon maple extract
- 4 slices bacon

Directions:

1. First the topping must be prepared. In a medium bowl, blend in sugar, flour, cinnamon, walnuts and butter. Using your fingers, blend in the butter until there are no pieces bigger than a little pea. Cover and refrigerate until prepared to use. Set up the cupcakes: Preheat your stove to 350°F. Line a 12-cup biscuit tin with paper liners. In an enormous bowl, whisk together the flour, sugar, preparing powder, cinnamon, allspice, nutmeg, and salt. Put in a safe spot. In a huge bowl utilizing an electric blender, beat together the cannabutter, cream, eggs, and maple syrup on medium speed until the blend is mixed well. Lessen the blender speed to low and include the flour blend. Beat until simply consolidated. Fill each well of the biscuit tin 2/3 full, bake it for around 20 to 25 minutes or until a toothpick embedded into the focal point of a cupcake tells the truth. While the cupcakes are heating, cook the bacon as how you like it done. Move to a paper towel to drip the excess oil and let cool. Cupcakes must be chilled off in the tin for around 15 minutes. At that point, move to a wire rack to cool totally. Cut the bacon into 12 pieces and press a piece into the top of each muffin. For storing muffins in the freezer, seal it tightly, and it can last up to 3 months, just omit the bacon. Reheat in the toaster oven for extra deliciousness.

Nutrition:

Calories: 190 Fat: 5g Fiber: 3g Carbs: 28.8g Protein: 1.7g

Cannabis Hummingbird Cupcakes

Preparation Time: 10-15 minutes

Cooking Time: 15-20 minutes

Servings: 12

Ingredients:

- 2 large ripe bananas, mashed
- 1 cup of all-purpose
- 1/2 tsp. baking powder
- 1/3 cup pineapple (crushed (do not drain)
- 1/2 tsp. baking soda
- 1/2 tsp. ground cinnamon
- 1/4 tsp. salt
- ½ cup cannabutter, at room temperature
- 1/2 cup sugar
- 2 large eggs
- 1 tsp. pure vanilla extract
- 1/2 cup chopped pecans

- 1 cup unsweetened desiccated coconut
- 1/2 cup golden raisins (optional)
- Cream Cheese Frosting
- 8 ounces cream cheese, at room temperature
- 1/4 cup butter, at room temperature
- 3 cups powdered sugar
- 2 teaspoons vanilla extract

Directions:

1. Preheat your oven to 350 degrees placing the rack in the center. Line a 12-cup muffin pan with cupcake liners in preparation. Combine the bananas and pineapples in a bowl. Mash together with the back of a fork and set aside. Whisk or beat together the flour, baking powder, baking soda, cinnamon and salt in a separate medium bowl. Add the cannabutter and the sugar to a large bowl. Beat with a whisk until the mixture is fluffy and light. Gradually put the eggs and then the vanilla extract. Add the dry ingredients into the wet by scoopfuls and beat until thoroughly combined.
2. Stir in the pineapple and bananas, being careful not to over-mix. Fold in the pecans, coconut and golden raisins (if using). Pour batter into the liners, working to fill at least 2/3 of the way. Put it inside the oven and let it bake for around 30 to 40 minutes. The signs of completed cupcakes will include a toothpick that comes out clean and an outwardly golden appearance.
3. Remove from the oven and place on a wire rack to cool. Once this is achieved, use a small spatula or kitchen knife to frost tops of each cupcake. Top with finely chopped pecans.
4. Frosting (Cream-cheese)
5. Put the cream cheese and the butter in a bowl then and beat together with a whisk until very smooth and no lumps. Then add in the vanilla extract and fine sugar, continuously beating until it is light and smooth.

Nutrition:

Calories: 216 Fat: 3.1g Fiber: 1.4g Carbs: 56g Protein: 4

Kirsch Chocolate Muffins

Preparation Time: 15 minutes

Cooking Time: 20-25 minutes

Servings: 6-8

Ingredients:

- 1/2 tsp. baking soda
- 1/2 cup of cannabutter
- ½ cup of roughly cut dark chocolate
- 3/4 cup of brown sugar
- 1/4 cup of either unsweetened cocoa powder (Dutch cocoa works too)
- 3/4 cup of milk
- 1 1/4 cups of self-rising flour
- 2 eggs
- 15 ounces of dark cherries in syrup (thawed, drained, whatever the preference)
- 1 tbsp. cocoa

- Extra 1 tsp. icing sugar

Directions:

1. Set the oven to 350°F. Prepare a 12-hole muffin tray with liners. Cream the butter and sugar together, adding a single egg at a time. Take the baking soda, the cocoa, and the flour and sift together with the butter mix from before. Finish up by combining with the milk, chocolate, and cherries. Try to fill each cupcake tin to approximately ¾ full and place in the preheated oven for 20-25 minutes. A sign that cupcakes are done is by doing the clean toothpick test. Once it is cooked, put it away from heat and let cool while the icing is made. Frost and enjoy it!

Nutrition:

Calories: 196 Fat: 4.2g Fiber: 1.8 Carbs: 30.6g Protein: 1.1g

Canna- Banana Crumble Muffins

Preparation Time: 10-15 minutes

Cooking Time: 18-20 minutes

Servings: 8-10

Ingredients:

- 1 ½ cups flour
- 1/3 cup cannabis butter
- 3 mashed bananas
- 3/4 cup cane sugar
- 1/3 cup packed brown sugar
- 1 tsp. baking soda
- 1 tsp. baking powder
- 1/2 tsp. table salt
- 1 egg
- 2 tbsp. flour
- 1 tbsp. butter
- 1/8 tsp. ground cinnamon

Directions:

1. Bring the heat of your oven to 350 f. and lightly butter a 10-cup muffin tray. Get out a large mixing bowl and mix the 1.5 cups flour, baking soda, baking powder and salt. In a separate bowl, mix the mashed bananas, egg, cane sugar and 1/3 cup melted cannabis butter. Stir this mixture into the first mixture until just blended. Spread this batter evenly into the greased or buttered muffin cups. In another bowl, combine the brown sugar, cinnamon and 2 tbsp. Flour. Cut in 1 tbsp. Butter. Sprinkle this mixture over the muffin batter in the trays. Bake 18 - 20 minutes; allow cooling on a wire rack and enjoying.

Nutrition:

Calories: 210 Fat: 6g Fiber: 2.4 Carbs: 35g Protein: 1.7 g

Cannabis Pancakes

Ingredients:
- 1/2 cup cannabis milk
- 1/2 cup whole milk
- 1 cup all purpose flour
- 2 tablespoons white sugar
- 2 teaspoons baking powder
- 1 egg beaten
- 2 tablespoons vegetable oil
- 1 teaspoon salt

Directions :
1. In a large bowl, mix flour, sugar, baking powder and salt. Make a well in the center, and pour in cannabis milk, whole milk, egg and oil. Mix until smooth.
2. Heat a lightly oiled griddle or frying pan over medium-high heat. Pour or scoop the batter onto the griddle, using approximately 1/4 cup for each pancake. Brown on both sides and serve hot.

3. Serve the cannabis pancakes.

Cannabis Carrot Cake

Ingredients:
- 1 cup cannabis milk
- 3 eggs
- 1 1/2 cups sugar
- 2 cups all-purpose flour
- 2 teaspoons baking soda
- 2 cups shredded carrots
- 1 cup flaked coconut
- 1 cup chopped walnuts
- 1 can crushed pineapple with juice
- 1 cup raisins
- 2 teaspoons vanilla extract
- 2 teaspoons ground cinnamon
- 1/4 teaspoon salt

Directions:

1. Preheat oven to 350 degrees F.

2. Grease and flour an 8×12 inch pan .

3. In a medium bowl, sift together flour, baking soda, salt and cinnamon. Set aside.

4. In a large bowl, combine eggs, cannabis milk, oil, sugar and vanilla. Mix well. Add flour mixture and mix well.

5. In a medium bowl, combine shredded carrots, coconut, walnuts, pineapple and raisins.

6. Using a large wooden spoon or a very heavy whisk, add carrot mixture to batter and fold in well.

7. Pour into prepared 8×12 inch pan, and bake for 1 hour. Check for doneness with toothpick.

8. Allow to cool for at least 20 minutes before serving.

Marijuana Cheesecake

Ingredients:

- 2 tablespoons cannabis butter

- 1 tablespoon normal butter

- 24 oreo cookies, divided

- 3 (250 grams) Philadelphia cream cheese packets

- 3/4 cup sugar

- 1 teaspoon vanilla 3 eggs

Directions:

1. Preheat oven to 330 degrees F.

2. Place 16 of the cookies in resealable plastic bag. Flatten bag to remove excess air, then seal bag. Finely crush cookies by rolling a rolling pin across the bag .

3. Place in bowl. Add butter; mix well. Press firmly onto bottom of 9-inch springform pan.

4. Beat cream cheese, sugar and vanilla in large bowl with electric mixer on medium speed until well blended. Add eggs, 1 at a time, beating just until blended after each addition.

5. Chop or crush remaining 8 cookies. Gently stir half of the chopped cookies into cream cheese batter. Pour over prepared crust; sprinkle with the remaining chopped cookies.

6. Bake 45 minutes or until center is almost set. Cool. Refrigerate 3 hours or overnight. Cut into 12 pieces. Store leftover cheesecake in refrigerator.

Cannabis Gingerbread

Ingredients:

- 1/4 cup cannabis butter

- 1/4 cup normal butter

- One egg

- One cup molasses

- 2 1/2 cups all-purpose flour

- 1 1/2 teaspoons bakins soda

- 1 teaspoon ground cumin

- 1 teaspoon ground ginger

- 1/2 teaspoon salt

- 1 cup hot water

Directions:
1. Preheat oven to 330 degrees F.
2. Grease and flour a 9-inch square pan.

3. In a large bowl, cream together the sugar and butter. Beat in the egg, and mix in the molasses.

4. In a bowl, sift together the flour, baking soda, salt, cinnamon, ginger and cloves. Blend into the creamed mixture. Stir in the hot water. Pour into the prepared pan.

5. Bake 1 hour in the preheated oven until a knife inserted in the center comes out clean. Allow to cool in pan before serving.

Chocolate Cannabis Bar

Ingredients:
- 1/4 cup cannabis butter

- 4 cups chocolate

Directions:
1. Melt the chocolate in a clean, dry bowl set over a pan of barely simmering water. If you want to temper the chocolate, add your cannabis butter.
2. Once the chocolate is melted (and tempered, if tempering the chocolate), remove the bowl from the pan and wipe the moisture off the bottom of the bowl.

3. Pour or spoon a layer of chocolate into your molds. Rap them on the counter a few times to distribute the chocolate evenly and release any air bubbles; then working quickly, top with any kinds of nuts, dried fruits or other ingredients that you wish and press them in slightly.

4. (You can also stir ingredients into the chocolate, such as toasted nuts, seeds, crisped rice cereal, snipped marshmallows or other ingredients, then pour the mixture into the molds.)

5. Immediately put the bars in the refrigerator until firm. If tempered chocolate is used, it shouldn't take more than five minutes for them to firm up. Otherwise, the chocolate will take longer.

Cannabis Basic Muffins

Ingredients:

- 1/4 cup melted cannabis butter

- 2 cups all-purpose flour

- 3 teaspoons baking powder

- 1/2 teaspoon salt

- 3/4 cup white sugar

- 1 egg

- 1 cup milk

Directions:

1. Preheat oven to 350 degrees F.
2. Melt cannabis butter on very low temperature .

3. Stir together the flour, baking powder, salt and sugar in a large bowl. Make a well in the center. In a small bowl or 2 cup measuring cup, beat egg with a fork. Stir in milk and cannabis butter. Pour all at once into the well in the flour mixture.

4. Mix quickly and lightly with a fork until moistened.The batter will be lumpy. Pour the batter into paper lined muffin pan cups.

5. Bake for 25 minutes or until golden.

Chewy Chocolate Chip Weed Cookies

Ingredients:

- 1/4 cup softened cannabis butter

- 1/2 cup softened normal butter

- 2 cups all-purpose flour

- 1/2 teaspoon baking soda

- 1/2 teaspoon salt

- One cup brown sugar

- 1/2 cup white suga r

- 1 tablespoon vanilla extract

- 1 egg

- 1 egg yolk

- 2 cups chocolate chips

Directions:

1. Preheat the oven to 325 degrees F.
2. Grease cookie sheets or line with parchment paper.

3. In a bowl, sift together the flour, baking soda and salt; set aside.

4. In a medium bowl, cream together the cannabis butter, normal butter, brown sugar and white sugar until well blended. Beat in the vanilla, egg and egg yolk until light and creamy.

5. Mix in the sifted ingredients until just blended. Stir in the chocolate chips by hand using a wooden spoon.

6. Drop cookie dough 1/4 cup at a time onto the prepared cookie sheets. Cookies should be about 3 inches apart.

7. Bake for 15 to 17 minutes in the preheated oven, or until the edges are lightly toasted. Cool on baking sheets for a few minutes before transferring to wire racks to cool completely.

Peanut Butter Bud Bars

Ingredients:
- ½ cup cannabutter, melted
- ½ cup regular butter, melted
- 1 tablespoon decarb seasoning
- 2 cups Graham cracker crumbs
- 2 cups powdered sugar
- 1 cup + 4 tablespoons creamy peanut butter
- 1 ½ cups semisweet chocolate chips

Directions:
1. In a bowl, mix cannabutter, regular butter, Graham cracker crumbs, powdered sugar and 1 cup creamy peanut butter until combined. Press evenly into bottom of 9×13 baking pan.
2. In a saucepan and on medium heat, mix the chocolate chips, decarb seasoning and 4 tablespoons peanut butter until melted and combined.

3. Spread the peanut butter mixture evenly on the crust and refrigerate for 2 hours.

4. Cut into 1 inch squares before serving.

Chronic Apple Crisp

Ingredients:
- 10 cups apples, peeled, cored, and sliced
- 1 cup white sugar
- 1 cup + 1 tablespoon all-purpose flour

- 1 teaspoon ground cinnamon

- ½ cup water

- 1 cup quick cooking oats

- 1 cup brown sugar

- ¼ teaspoon baking powder

- ¼ teaspoon baking soda

- ½ cup cannabutter, melted

- 1 ounce cannabis tincture

Directions :
1. Heat oven to 350 degrees F. Spread apples evenly in 9×13 inch baking pan
2. In separate dish, mix cinnamon, 1 tablespoon flour and white sugar until combined. Sprinkle mix on apples. Pour water on apples.

3. In separate dish, mix oats, brown sugar, baking powder, baking soda, remaining flour, cannabutter and tincture until combined. Spread mixture evenly on top of apples'

4. Bake for 45 minutes. Serve warm.

Space Cake

Ingredients:
- 1 ¼ cups of baking flour

- 200 CL. of milk

- 2 eggs

- 180 grams of sugar

- ¾ cup butter

- 8 grams of good (light) hash. (You can use Polm or Zero.)

Directions:
1. Preheat oven to 200 degrees c
2. Put the butter in the microwave for about 20 seconds until it's a fat paste. Mix the hash with 4/5th of the butter. (Heat up the hash with a lighter and crumble it in the butter.) With the rest of the butter your fatten the baking form so you can get the cake out easy when it's done.

3. Mix the butter (and hash), flour, eggs, milk and sugar (and the possible extra ingredient). Keep on mixing it for a few minutes until it's nice and smooth. If it's too dry: add a little milk. If there is too much liquid, add a little flour.

Cannabis Sugar Cookies

Ingredients:
- 1 cup of cannabis butter
- 1 cup brown sugar
- 1/2 cup white sugar
- 1 large egg
- 1 teaspoon vanilla
- 2 cups all-purpose flour
- 1/2 teaspoon of baking powder
- Pinch or two of salt

Directions:

1. Preheat oven to

2. Place the cannabis butter in a large bowl, and beat until it is very light and fluffy .

3. Once fluffy, add sugar, a quarter cup at a time, continuing to vigorously beat the mix.

4. Beat in the large egg and the vanilla flavoring.

5. In a separate small bowl, mix together the baking powder, flour and the pinch of salt.

6. Gradually beat the flour mix into the large bowl until completely mixed together.

7. Divide the finished dough mixture into two halves, wrap each half in plastic wrap, and then refrigerate overnight.

8. Roll each half with a rolling pin on a floured surface; the dough should have a thickness of about ? of an inch.

9. Use a cookie cutter, any shape that you want, and then place the dough shapes onto a prepared cookie sheet at least 1 inch apart.

10. Bake for 10-12 minutes, remove them from the oven when they look golden brown.

11. Leave the cookies to cool before eating.

Strawberry Weed Muffins

Ingredients:
- 1 cup of flour
- 1/2 cup of quick oats
- 2 teaspoons of baking powder
- 1/4 cup of sugar
- 1/2 teaspoon of salt
- 1 large egg

- 1/4 cup of cannabis butter

- 1 cup of mil k

- 1 cup of fresh strawberries

Directions:
1. Preheat oven to 380F-400F.
2. Mix together the oats, flour, baking powder, sugar and salt in a large mixing bowl.

3. In a smaller bowl, mix together the egg, milk and marijuana butter.

4. Make a crater in the large bowl, and then pour in the liquid mix from the smaller bowl.

5. Stir it up a little - don't stir until smooth - it should be lumpy.

6. Carefully insert the strawberries deep into the mix; you can slice the strawberries into halves and quarters if you wish.

7. Pour the mixture into a muffin tin, using muffin liners, make sure that you leave room in each muffin tin for them to rise. Your mix should fill about 75% of the capacity of the liners.

8. Bake for 25-30 minutes in an oven.

9. Leave to cool on a wire rack, and then enjoy!

Adult Weed Brownies

Ingredients:
- 1/4 pound butter

- 1/4 pound dark chocolate

- 1 cup of white sugar

- 4 regular eggs

- 1/2 cup plain flour

- Nutmeg

- Cinnamon

- 2 tablespoons of vanilla

- 1 ounce of finely ground cannabis bud (or 2-3 ounces of cannabis leaf, but is much better)

Directions :
1. Preheat your oven to 350 degrees F.
2. Melt the butter over a low heat, then add the chocolate (in cubes is quickest) and melt that in with the already melted butter; stir regularly so that it becomes chocolate butter!

3. As soon as the chocolate has melted entirely, add the cinnamon, nutmeg and the white sugar; stir and simmer for a few minutes.

4. Add the eggs, one at a time, beating them so that the yolk breaks up. Continue to stir the mixture on a low heat until it is completely smooth.

5. Add the flour and finely ground cannabis to the mix. If you like nuts, then you can add a quarter of a cup of your favorite nut if you wish. Stir it well; if it is difficult to stir, then add a small dash of milk.

6. Pour your mixture into a greased 9x13 inch pan - if you don't have one then a smaller one is OK – it just means a thicker brownie and possibly a little longer in the oven.

7. Bake your mixture for 20-25 minutes, sometimes a little longer is required.

8. Once it looks and feels like a giant brownie, cut it into around 20 square. It doesn't matter how many squares, of course.

9. Dosage: Wait an hour and see how you feel. Then eat more as required! These brownies taste delicious and it is difficult to resist eating them, but you don't want to eat too many and then whitey!

Cannabombs

Items Need:
- Medium sized pot
- Small ceramic dish
- Aluminum Foil
- Oven bag (the kind used for cooking)
- Baking sheet
- Candy thermometer
- Wax paper
- Cheesecloth, optional (needed for larger quantities of herb)
- *Double boiler
- 5 grams of hash or 14 grams of herb
  - (*If using a microwave chocolate, add the additional canna oil in the peanut butter and increase powder sugar accordingly - the double boiler pots are no longer required, unless making herb oil rather than hash oil.)

3
- 2/3 cup peanut butter
- 2 – 2 ½ cups confectioners' sugar
- ½ teaspoon vanilla extract
- 1/2 cup butter and/or coconut oil – you can get away with less oil by using hash; this way, you won't dilute the peanut butter flavor quite so much with oil and sugar.

For Chocolate Coating:

- Any hard, dark Bakers melting chocolate or chips, roughly ¾ – 1 cup.

- 2/3 teaspoon coconut hash oil (works better than the butter alternative, but use no other oil)

- Paraffin/baking wax

<u>Optional (recommended):</u>
- Lecithin powder

<u>Optional (for "fuse"):</u>
- Thick, cotton cooking string, or white yarn

- Paraffin wax

- Ceramic dish or a small home-made 'foil bowl'

Directions :
1. Preheat oven to 200 degrees F.
2. Cut 20 x 2 ½" sections of thick white string or yarn (you may need spares). Tie a small knot at one end of each string.

3. In oven, melt a small portion of paraffin wax in a small ceramic dish, takes only 2 – 3 minutes… it can be very carefully microwaved, or heated slowly on the stove-top, but it's MUCH, much safer and more controlled in the oven, and at a set temperature.

4. Carefully remove the paraffin from the oven with a potholder - it will be very warm - so set it on a safe surface. Begin dipping the strings, tied end first, into the paraffin, coating the yarn well. If heated in the oven at 200, it should be cool enough to grab by the opposite end once dipped, to flip and coat the entire string. Be quick, or you'll be reheating your paraffin a few times! The wax helps keep the ball formed around the string, and it also prevents stray strands of string fiber from being eaten by you, your patients or your guests.

5. Now you are ready to add your oils and lecithin.

6. You can use a combination of oils, both for flavor and to create a varied oil 'vehicle' for cannabinoid bonding and availability, some thinner and some thicker. In the end, you want it to be a solid at room temp, so your canna balls aren't too soft, and the chocolate keeps its shape and thickness. The additional liquid oils used in addition to the solids had previously been infused with herb.

7. Ideally, you should be using butter and/or coconut oil, about 1 ½ tablespoons worth for your hash. If this is your primary or only canna oil source, you'll be adding an additional 2 tablespoons of softened butter to the peanut butter filling later on.

8. And your double boiler, with your melted oils and lecithin over a low heat.

9. (You can use slightly more oil, knowing that with this much herb, a small but noticeable quantity of oil will be left behind.)

10. Cover tight with foil using the foil to seal the thermometer in place; keep between 180-200 degrees F, turning off the heat periodically as it rises. This is what it looks like after about ten or so hours:

11. Allow to cool somewhat, so it's only warm to the touch, and set up your cheesecloth.

12. Now, you can begin straining.

13. When using this much green for such a small amount of oil, I know there will be some potent material left within the herb that is worth keeping, so save and freeze the green for a future run, and use only the oil.

14. However, knowing you'll be using a smaller amount, and if it was initially ground finely enough, you can choose to add it all directly to the peanut butter.

 Now with one (or both) of these oils, you're finally ready to make the peanut butter balls!

For the Peanut Butter Balls:

1. In a mixing bowl, you'll be blending your peanut butter, vanilla and all your canna oil- except for roughly 2/3 teaspoon which will go in the chocolate - only if made with butter and/or coconut oil; otherwise, use it all in the peanut butter. If only using hash oil, remember to add a few tablespoons of additional butter at this point.
2. Once that is done, you should have an oily peanut butter goo, and you're ready to begin mixing in your powdered sugar until it reaches a consistency that will hold shape and not crumble.

Making the Peanut Butter Centers Using the 'Fuse':

1. Cover the base of a cookie sheet or baking pan with foil or wax paper .
2. Take enough peanut butter filling, so that when rolled, it should create roughly a 1 1/4 – 1 1/2 inch diameter ball.

3. Once it's balled up, insert the 'fuse' about half-way through the ball, KNOT-END FIRST, then gently squeeze and reform the ball making sure that it's stable.

4. If you'd like, you can place them down gently but firmly on the foil or wax paper, just enough to create a 'flat' on the very base to keep them from rolling around.

5. Having the fuse-knot in the center holds it in very snug, and prevents the fuse from slipping around and falling out, or crumbling the peanut butter; you can carefully bend the fuse so it looks decorative, or more 'cartoon-ish'.

6. Pop the tray into the freezer for no longer than 20 minutes while you complete the following.

For Chocolate Coating:

1. This can be as simple or tedious as you like. If you're not adept in the kitchen or familiar with tempering chocolate, I recommend using all your hash/canna oil in the peanut butter ball portion, disregard the double boiler, and use one of the newer, more simple microwavable melting chocolates, which are designed for easy, consistent use .
2. Otherwise, you may be frustrated when the consistency fails, and it's more of a lumpy sauce than a coating.

3. Using a double boiler pot, grab a handful of semisweet, dark and milk chocolate baking chips, concentrating on the dark and semisweet, and slowly melt them over the lowest heat possible.

4. Once the chocolate is melted, add hash oil, blend and then begin shaving small amounts of paraffin into the chocolate. You will have to blend again, then drop a little on wax paper. Once it stays nice and solid, it's ready. Remove from heat.

5. If you choose to make your own chocolate coat but without adding additional canna oil, there is no need for the paraffin; just temper as usual, and they will be much shinier this way. Remember the smaller and taller the pot, the easier it will be to use as a coat.

6. Remove your peanut butter balls from the freezer (or the refrigerator, if you waited longer than 20 minutes), and grab them one at a time by the fuse.

7. Quickly dunk each ball in the cooling chocolate, and place on your wax paper. A new sheet can be used, or you can carefully return each ball to the last sheet.

8. The cold temperature of the peanut butter ball will rapidly solidify the cooling chocolate. This is why it's best to work fast and use the freezer rather than the fridge for the ball; the outer edge becomes colder than it can in the fridge without allowing the center to become frozen (which can cause crumbling/cracking in the center around the fuse when dunked into the warm chocolate).

9. After dunking each ball, take a spoon. Using the excess chocolate, place a small drop on the end of each fuse… now they're lit.

10. Pop them in the freezer, and you're done!

Hot Canna Cocoa

Time: 25 minutes

Serving Size: 4 servings
Prep Time: 5 minutes
Cook Time: 20 minutes

Ingredients:
- 6 ounces water
- 3 cups whole milk
- 3 tablespoons unsweetened cocoa powder
- 6 ounces finely chopped semi-sweet chocolate or semi-sweet chocolate chips
- 3 tablespoons sugar
- 1 teaspoon cannabis butter or a few drops of cannabis tincture

Equipment:
- Saucepan
- Whisk
- Mugs

Directions:
1. Place the saucepan with the water in it over medium-high heat and let it come to a simmer.

2. Add the cocoa powder and whisk until smooth without lumps.

3. Whisk in the milk and bring the mixture back up to a simmer but not a boil.

4. Add in the sugar and chocolate and continue to whisk for a further five minutes, until the chocolate is completely melted and the whole mixture is creamy and smooth.

5. Pour the hot cocoa into the mugs and stir a teaspoon of cannabis butter into each mug. Alternatively, you can skip the butter and opt to add a few drops of cannabis tincture to your cocoa instead.

Lemonade

Time: 1 hour 30 minutes

Serving Size: 8 servings
Prep Time: 3o minutes

Cook Time: 1 hour

Ingredients:
- ½ cup of freshly squeezed lemon juice
- 3 ¼ cups water
- ¼ cup cranberry juice cocktail
- ⅔ cups of sugar
- 4 tablespoons cannabis tincture (Start with half the tincture to test the potency. You can add more as desired.)

Equipment:
- Saucepan
- Large airtight container

Directions:
1. Place the saucepan with one cup of water in it over medium-high heat, then add the sugar to the saucepan. Dissolve the sugar by stirring and bring the mix up to a boil.

2. Once sugar is dissolved, allow the syrup to cool on a counter until it reaches room temperature. Transfer to an airtight container and refrigerate until chilled.

3. Combine the syrup and all the other ingredients in a large pitcher and serve your pink cannabis-infused lemonade chilled over ice cubes.

Marijuana Milkshake

Time: 10 minutes

Serving Size: 1 serving
Prep Time: 5 minutes
Cook Time: 5 minutes

Ingredients:
- 2 teaspoons cannabis tincture (Start with half the tincture or only a few drops and increase the dose as desired.)
- 1 cup fresh or frozen strawberries
- 1 teaspoon vanilla extract
- 3/4 cup milk
- 1 cup strawberry ice cream

Equipment:
- Blender

Directions:
1. Place all the ingredients into the blender and blend well until incorporated and the milkshake has a smooth consistency.

2. Pour into a mug or glass of your choice and enjoy.

Thai Iced Tea

Time: 15 minutes

Serving Size: 6 servings

Prep Time: 5 minutes
Cook Time: 10 minutes

Ingredients:
- 6 chai tea bags (If you don't have chai tea, you can substitute 6 black tea bags and add in ½ teaspoon of ground cinnamon, one star anise pod, two cardamom pods, and ½ teaspoon vanilla extract.)
- 8 cups boiling water
- 1 14-ounce can condensed milk
- 3 to 5 tablespoons melted cannabis butter
- Optional: ¼ to ½ cup granulated sugar

Equipment:
- Large pitcher
- Small mixing bowl
- 6 glasses

Directions:
1. Place your tea bags and spices in a large pitcher and pour in the boiling water. Allow the tea to steep for approximately four to five minutes before removing the tea bags and any whole spices.

2. Set the tea aside and allow it to cool down to room temperature.

3. While the tea is cooling, mix together the cannabutter and the condensed milk and set aside.

4. To serve, fill the six glasses with ice cubes, or half-fill them with crushed ice. Pour the tea into each glass, filling only two-thirds of a glass. Top it all off with two ounces of the condensed milk mixture. The condensed milk mix will sink to the bottom. Stir it all up and enjoy it.

The Proper Pineapple Smoothie

Time: 10 minutes

Serving Size: 2 servings
Prep Time: 5 minutes
Cook Time: 5 minutes

Ingredients:
- 2 tablespoons cannabis-infused coconut oil
- 1 cup frozen sliced pineapple
- ¼ cup sliced banana
- ½ cup water
- ½ cup milk
- 1 teaspoon chia seeds (optional)

Equipment:
- Blender

Directions:
1. Pack the banana and pineapple into the blender and pour in the water and milk. Blend the lot together until you have achieved a smooth consistency.

2. Gradually and slowly add the two tablespoons of canna coconut oil and blend until well incorporated.

3.   Serve the pineapple smoothie in two glasses and top with chia seeds if you'd like.

Mayonnaise

Time: 2 hours 10 minutes
Serving Size: 2 cups of canna mayo
Prep Time: 10 minutes

Cook Time: 2 hours

Ingredients:
- 3 egg yolks
- 1 cup cannabis oil
- ½ teaspoon Dijon mustard
- 1 teaspoon white vinegar
- 1 teaspoon fresh lemon juice
- A pinch of sea salt

Equipment:
- 1 medium-sized bowl
- Whisk
- 1 appropriately-sized canning jar with a lid

Directions:
1.   In a medium-sized bowl, whisk together all of the ingredients, except the cannabis oil, until they are well incorporated.

2.   Keep whisking and gradually pour the cannaoil into the mixture.

3.   Whisk the lot until the mayonnaise starts to get thicker. If it becomes too thick, you can add a few drops of water which will thin it out to your ideal consistency.

4.   Pour the canna mayo into the canning jar and allow it to cool to room temperature before sealing and storing it in the fridge.

Caesar Salad Dressing

Time: 20 minutes
Serving Size: 2 cups of salad dressing
Prep Time: 10 minutes
Cook Time: 10 minutes

Ingredients:
- 1 ½ cups cannabis oil
- 2 eggs
- 10 cloves of garlic
- ½ cup lemon juice
- 2 teaspoons sea salt

Equipment:
- A small saucepan
- 1 canning jar with a lid

Directions:

1. Pour the water into the saucepan and bring to a boil over medium to high heat.

2. Place the eggs in the water and boil them for 30 seconds. This pasteurizes the eggs.

3. Crack the eggs and combine in a blender with all the other ingredients except the cannaoil. Blend the concoction for approximately one minute.

4. Keep the blender switched on while slowly adding the cannabis oil to the mixture until everything is well blended.

5. Pour the salad dressing into the jar, seal, and store in the fridge.

6. Give the jar a good shake before serving to mix any ingredients that may have sunken to the bottom of the jar.

Lemon Vinaigrette

Time: 15 minutes
Serving Size: Approximately 1 ¼ cups of vinaigrette
Prep Time: 10 minutes
Cook Time: 5 minutes

Ingredients:
- ¼ cup cannabis olive oil
- ¾ cup extra-virgin olive oil
- ¼ cup fresh lemon juice
- ¼ teaspoon honey
- 1 teaspoon minced garlic
- 1 teaspoon dried oregano

Equipment:
- Blender
- 1 bottle or canning jar with a lid

Directions:

1. Throw all of the ingredients to your blender, switch it on, and blend until everything is well incorporated. That's it – super simple and easy-to-make vinaigrette.

2. Pour the cannabis-infused vinaigrette into a bottle or jar and store it in the fridge.

3. Give the vinaigrette a good shake before use to mix up any ingredients that may have sunken to the bottom.

BBQ Sauce

Time: 3 hours 10 minutes
Serving Size: 2 cups of sauce
Prep Time: 10 minutes

Cook Time: 3 hours

Ingredients:
- ⅓ ounce of average decarboxylated cannabis
- ⅓ cup vegetable oil

- Juice of 1 lime
- 2 tablespoons Worcestershire sauce
- 2 tablespoons apple cider vinegar
- 1 tablespoons soy sauce
- ¾ tomato paste
- 1 tablespoon honey
- ½ cup apricot nectar
- ¼ cup water
- 2 tablespoons dark brown sugar
- 1 tablespoon fresh minced garlic
- 3 tablespoons of chopped green onion
- ½ tablespoons chili powder
- A pinch of cayenne pepper
- A pinch of ground ginger

Equipment:
- A crockpot
- 1 canning jar with a lid

Directions:
1. Finely crumble the cannabis and put it in a crockpot, along with the water and lime juice. Cook for around two hours.

2. Add the rest of the ingredients to the crockpot and mix well until everything is incorporated.

3. Cook for an additional hour, stirring regularly.

4. Pour your cannabis BBQ sauce into the canning jar and allow it to cool to room temperature before sealing. Store your sauce in the fridge and give it a shake before use so that any ingredients that sink to the bottom get mixed up again.

Pesto

Time: 15 minutes
Serving Size: Approximately 1 cup of pesto
Prep Time: 10 minutes
Cook Time: 5 minutes

Ingredients:
- Walnuts
- ¼ cup freshly grated Parmesan cheese
- 1 cup cannabis-infused olive oil
- 2 cloves garlic
- 2 cups basil
- A pinch of sea salt

Equipment:
- 1 canning jar with a lid
- Blender
- Saucepan

Directions:

1. Use medium heat to warm up a skillet and toast the pine nuts. This will take approximately three minutes. Keep stirring the nuts to prevent them from burning.

2. Take the saucepan off the heat and let the pine nuts cool down.

3. Put the pine nuts in your blender and blend on high until they are ground up to resemble a coarse flour.

4. Rinse the basil off and pat dry with a paper towel before removing the stems and breaking the leaves into small pieces.

5. Add all of the remaining ingredients except the cannaoil to the ground pine nuts in the blender.

6. Switch the processor on medium to low speed and, while it's blending the ingredients, gradually add 1/3 of the cup of cannaoil. Add the basil, garlic, salt, and Parmesan to the walnut flour in the food processor.

7. Taste the pesto and add more salt or cannaoil until the taste and consistency is to your liking.

Sriracha Hot Sauce

Time: 24 hours
Serving Size: Approximately 1 cup of sriracha sauce
Prep Time: 10 minutes

Cook Time: 24 hours

Ingredients:
- ½ cup cannabis cooking oil
- 8 cloves of garlic
- 12 hot chili peppers of your choice (The hotter the peppers, the hotter your siracha will be.)
- ¼ cup apple cider vinegar
- 3 tablespoons of honey (You can use cannabis-infused honey for an extra kick if you like.)

Equipment:
- Aluminum foil
- A baking sheet
- A blender/food processor
- 1 canning jar with a lid

Directions:
1. Switch your oven on and preheat it to 350° F.

2. Cover the baking sheet with aluminum foil so that every inch of it is covered.

3. Lay the chili peppers on the foil-covered sheet and roast them for 10 minutes.

4. Remove the sheet from the oven and rotate the peppers.

5. Spread the garlic evenly on the baking sheet and return it to the oven to bake for a further 10 minutes.

6. Remove the baking sheet from the oven and allow the peppers and garlic to cool until you can handle them without burning your fingers. Remove the stems from the chili peppers.

7. Put the peppers and garlic into the food processor along with the rest of the ingredients. You can also always add some more garlic if you like a lot of garlic.

8. Turn that blender on and keep going until everything is blended together and your sriracha sauce has a smooth consistency. If you like it a bit chunkier, simply blend until the sauce reaches your desired chunkiness.

9. Pour the sauce into the canning jar and allow it to cool completely.

10. Seal the jar and store in the fridge. Allow your sriracha sauce to sit for 24 hours before you use it so that all the flavors meld together.

Nacho Cheese Sauce

Time: 25 minutes

Serving Size: Serves 6
Prep Time: 5 minutes
Cook Time: 20 minutes

Ingredients:
- 2 tablespoons cannabis butter
- 1 cup whole milk at room temperature
- 2 tablespoons flour
- 1 ½ cup shredded/grated cheddar cheese
- ¼ teaspoon salt (or to taste)
- ¼ teaspoon pepper (or to taste)
- Optional extras: a pinch of cayenne/cumin/garlic powder

Equipment:
- A skillet
- Whisk

Directions:
1. Use medium heat to get the skillet warmed up and melt the cannabis-infused butter.

2. Add in the flour and whisk well. The mixture should become crumb-like or even form a paste.

3. Slowly and gradually add the milk while whisking like crazy to smooth out the mixture and break up any lumps. Keep whisking away as the mixture reaches a simmer.

4. Sprinkle in cheddar cheese a bit at a time. Don't add too much at once, and spread it out to avoid cheese lumps.

5. Keep whisking – nacho cheese dip requires a lot of whisking and a good whisking arm. As you add cheese to the dipping sauce, allow the previous lot to melt completely before adding more.

6. Add the seasonings that you prefer to use for this dip.

7. Enjoy the cheesy goodness immediately – do not refrigerate and reheat it, as this spoils the texture.

Peanut Butter

Time: 10 minutes

Serving size: 1 serving

Prep time: 5 minutes
Cook Time: 5 minutes

Ingredients:
* 2 tablespoons peanut butter of your choice
* 2 teaspoons cannabis infused cooking oil

Equipment:
* Spoon
* Bowl

Directions:
1. Combine the cannabis oil infusion and the peanut butter in a small bowl and stir well until thoroughly incorporated.

2. If the consistency is not thick enough, chill in the fridge for a short while to stiffen the peanut butter up.

Hummus

Time: 10 minutes
Serving size: 1 cup of hummus
Prep time: 5 minutes
Cook Time: 5 minutes

Ingredients:
* 7.5 ounces of cooked chickpeas (also called garbanzo beans)
* 1/8 cup tahini
* 1/8 cup of freshly squeezed lemon juice, strained
* 2 cloves of garlic, fresh
* ½ an ounce to 1 ounce of cannabis-infused cooking oil such as canola or olive oil (the amount you add will depend on how potent you want the hummus to be)
* ¼ teaspoon cumin, ground
* 1 to 2 tablespoons of water
* Salt and pepper to taste

Equipment:
* Blender or food processor
* Bowl

Directions:
1. Using a blender or a food processor, mix the tahini and the lemon juice together and blend for about 30 seconds.

2. Add in all of the remaining ingredients but only half of the water and blend the lot together well until you have a smooth texture. This will take approximately one minute.

3. If the hummus is too stiff or thick, add a little bit more water and blend again until you reach the consistency you want.

4. Pour the hummus from the blender or processor into a serving or dipping bowl and enjoy.

Gummy Sweets

Time: 45 minutes

Serving Size: 12 servings
Prep Time: 5 minutes
Cook Time: 40 minutes

Ingredients:
- 2 tablespoons unflavored plain gelatin
- 1 3-ounce package of flavored Jell-O
- ½ cup canna coconut oil
- ½ cup of cold water
- ½ teaspoon of soy or sunflower lecithin (optional)

Equipment:
- Whisk
- Cooking pot
- Ladle or dropper
- Gummy bear mold or another food-safe mold of your choice

Directions:
1. Put a pot over low heat and add the water, canna coconut oil, and the lecithin if you're using it.
2. Allow the mixture to heat up, stirring constantly, until the oil has melted.
3. Stir in the unflavored and flavored gelatins.
4. Continue whisking the mixture for about 10 to 15 minutes until the gelatin has been entirely dissolved and incorporated. Keep the heat low and do not allow the mixture to reach a boil.
5. Once the 15 minutes is up, use a dropper or a ladle to fill the molds. It is crucial to work quickly while filling the molds, as the mixture could start to cool and separate.
6. Keep whisking the mixture in the pot between pouring to keep the mixture well combined.
7. When a mold is filled, lift it off the countertop slightly and drop it to dislodge any air bubbles in your gummy mixture.
8. Transfer the molds to the freezer for approximately 25 minutes.

Tip: Toss the ganja gummies in cornstarch to prevent them from sticking together after removing them from the molds.

Cannabis Chocolate

Time: 25 minutes plus cooling time
Serving Size: Makes enough chocolate for 2 people
Prep Time: 10 minutes
Cook Time: 15 minutes

Ingredients:
- ⅛ cup cannabis-infused butter
- 1 cups chocolate
- Pieces of dried fruit or nuts (optional)

Equipment:

- Pot
- Glass bowl that fits onto the pot to create a makeshift double-boiler
- Chocolate bar molds or other food-safe molds
- Ladle

Directions:

1. Fill the pot halfway with water and bring to a gentle simmer over medium heat.

2. Put the chocolate into the glass bowl and place the bowl into the top of the pot so that the bottom is not touching the simmering water.

3. Put your cannabutter into the bowl with the chocolate and allow everything to melt completely, stirring to combine.

4. Ladle or pour the melted chocolate into the molds and rap the molds on the countertop to dislodge any air bubbles.

5. If you are adding fruit or nuts to your chocolate, do so now and press the pieces into the chocolate slightly.

6. Refrigerate your canna chocolate immediately until it is set and firm.

Chocolate Chip Canna Cookies

Time: 25 minutes
Serving size: Dependent on the size of the cookies
Prep time: 15 minutes
Cook Time: 10 minutes

Ingredients:

- 2 cups and 1/3 heaped cup all-purpose flour
- 3/4 cup granulated white sugar
- 1 cup granulated brown sugar
- 1 ounce regular butter
- 6 ounces cannabis-infused butter
- 2 large eggs
- 1 teaspoon baking soda
- 1 teaspoon salt
- 1 teaspoon vanilla extract
- 1 3/4 cups chocolate chips

Equipment:

- Baking sheets
- Non-stick cooking spray
- Large mixing bowl
- Large mixing spoon

Directions:

1. Spray your baking sheets with the non-stick spray and set them aside.

2. Turn your oven to 375° F and let it preheat while mixing the cookie dough.

3. In a small bowl, mix together the baking soda, flour, and salt.

4. In a large bowl, cream the regular and cannabis butter, sugars, and vanilla extract.

5. One at a time, add the eggs to the butter mixture and combine well.

6. Slowly add the flour mix to the butter mixture, stirring in one cup at a time.

7. Pour in the chocolate chips and stir to distribute them evenly throughout the dough.

8. Roll the dough into balls, arrange them on the baking sheets and flatten slightly.

9. Bake the cookies for between 9 and 11 minutes or until done.

Mallow Bars

Time: 30 minutes plus cooling time
Serving size: Dependent on the size of the mallow bars when cut
Prep time: 10 minutes
Cook Time: 20 minutes

Ingredients:
* 1 pack of marshmallows
* ¼ cup of cannabis butter
* 6 cups of Cinnamon Toast Crunch cereal, Rice Krispies, or Fruit Loops

Equipment:
* 13" x 9" x 2" pan
* Non-stick cooking spray or butter for greasing
* Large saucepan or pot

Directions:
1. Evenly coat the pan in non-stick spray or butter, making sure to get into the corners.

2. Using low heat, put the cannabutter in the saucepan and melt it. Stir to prevent burning.

3. Empty the entire bag of marshmallows into the saucepan. Stir the marshmallows and melted butter until all the marshmallows are fully melted.

4. Remove the saucepan from the heat and add in the cereal of your choice. Mix the whole lot together to evenly coat the cereal with the marshmallow mix.

5. Pour the mixture into the prepared pan, ensuring that it is evenly spread across the pan.

6. Press down firmly to compact the mixture so that it will hold its shape once set.

7. Allow the bars to cool at room temperature or pop them in the fridge to speed up the process. If you refrigerate them, allow them to warm up a little before slicing.

8. Slice the cereal bars into blocks according to your size preference.

Chocolate Canna Clusters

Time: 40 minutes plus cooling time
Serving size: Dependent on the size of the clusters
Prep time: 10 minutes
Cook Time: 30 minutes

Ingredients:

- 6 ounces of semi-sweet chocolate chips
- 1 1/2 cups chopped pecans
- 1/2 cup cannabis-infused butter
- 1 pinch salt
- 2/3 cup sweetened condensed milk
- 1 cup firmly packed light brown sugar
- 1/2 cup light corn syrup
- 1/2 teaspoon vanilla extract

Equipment:

- 2 baking sheets
- Non-stick cooking spray
- Saucepan
- Candy or cooking thermometer

Directions:

1. Grease the baking trays and arrange the chopped pecans in little clusters on the sheets. Spread them out evenly and set them aside.

2. Over medium heat, melt the cannabis butter in a saucepan. Once melted, stir in the sugar and salt until the sugar dissolves.

3. Add in the sweetened condensed milk and corn syrup and allow it to cook until the concoction reaches a temperature of 250° F. Use the thermometer to check the temperature of the mixture. Stir the mixture regularly to prevent burning. This should take around 15 to 20 minutes.

4. Add the vanilla extract and then place spoonfuls of the caramel mixture on top of the pecan clusters. Set the trays aside for the caramel to cool and harden.

5. Over medium-low to low heat, melt the chocolate chips carefully in a saucepan until the melted chocolate is smooth. Stir constantly to prevent burning.

6. Once the caramels have cooled and firmed up, you can either dip them in the chocolate, generously drizzle the chocolate over them, or spoon blobs of chocolate on top of them.

7. Set aside to cool completely and set the chocolate.

Granola Bars

Time: 25 minutes plus cooling time

Serving size: 16 bars
Prep time: 10 minutes
Cook Time: 15 minutes

Ingredients:

- 2 1/2 cups old-fashioned rolled oats
- 1/2 cup roughly chopped nuts (almonds, pecans, cashews)
- 1/4 cup honey
- 2 tablespoons cannabis-infused butter
- 2 tablespoons unsalted butter
- 1/3 cup brown sugar

- 1 teaspoon vanilla extract
- 3/4 cups additional ingredients of your choice

Options include:
- Sunflower seeds
- Shredded coconut
- Dried blueberries
- Dried cranberries
- Dried cherries
- Dried pineapple
- Dried mandarin oranges
- Dried mango
- Chopped-up pretzels
- Chocolate chips (dark chocolate, milk chocolate, semi-sweet, white chocolate)
- Peanut butter chips
- M&Ms
- Peanut butter M&Ms
- Chopped peppermint candy
- Reese's Pieces
- 1/4 cup peanut butter (If using peanut butter, only use ½ a cup of other add-ins.)

Equipment:
- 9" baking pan
- Non-stick cooking spray or parchment paper
- Large bowl
- Small saucepan

Directions:
1. Spray the pan with non-stick spray or line it with parchment paper to prevent sticking.

2. In a large bowl, mix the nuts and the oats.

3. Using medium heat, melt and mix together the honey, brown sugar, cannabis butter, and regular butter until the sugar has fully dissolved and everything is well combined. Stir regularly to prevent burning.

4. Remove from the heat and add in the salt and vanilla extract. If you are choosing to use ¼ cup of peanut butter, add this now. Stir everything together until well combined.

5. Pour this mixture over the nuts and oats in the bowl. Throw your add-ins into the bowl, as well except for any form of chocolate or chocolate-coated candy if you are using any.

6. Mix it all up until everything is well coated.

7. Let the mixture cool and then add chocolate if you are using any.

8. Pour the granola bar mix into the baking pan, spreading it evenly and pressing down firmly to compact the mixture for firmer bars that are less likely to fall apart.

9. Pop the pan into the fridge for a minimum of two hours or up to overnight.

10. Slice the granola into 16 bars, remove from the pan, and enjoy.
11. Store your ganja granola bars in the freezer.

Tips:

Lay the nuts and oats on a baking sheet, evenly spread out, and bake them for around eight or so minutes to lightly toast them. Toasting the oats and nuts will lend a cookie-like flavor to your granola bars. Crumble the granola bars over yogurt or into milk for a quick and tasty breakfast option.

Kirsch Chocolate Muffins

- Preparation Time: 15 minutes

- Cooking Time: 20-25 minutes

- Servings: 6-8

Ingredients:

- 1/2 tsp. baking soda

- 1/2 cup of cannabutter

- ½ cup of roughly cut dark chocolate

- 3/4 cup of brown sugar

- 1/4 cup of either unsweetened cocoa powder (Dutch cocoa works too)

- 3/4 cup of milk

- 1 1/4 cups of self-rising flour

- 2 eggs

- 15 ounces of dark cherries in syrup (thawed, drained, whatever the preference)

- 1 tbsp. cocoa

- Extra 1 tsp. icing sugar

Directions:

- Set the oven to 350°F. Prepare a 12-hole muffin tray with liners. Cream the butter and sugar together, adding a single egg at a time. Take the baking soda, the cocoa, and the flour and sift together with the butter mix from before. Finish up by combining with the milk, chocolate, and cherries. Try to fill each cupcake tin to approximately ¾ full and place in the preheated oven for 20-25 minutes. A sign that cupcakes are done is by doing the clean toothpick test. Once it is cooked, put it away from heat and let cool while the icing is made. Frost and enjoy it!

- **Nutrition:** Calories: 196 Fat: 4.2g Fiber: 1.8 Carbs: 30.6g Protein: 1.1g

Canna- Banana Crumble Muffins

- Preparation Time: 10-15 minutes

- Cooking Time: 18-20 minutes

- Servings: 8-10

Ingredients:

- 1 ½ cups flour

- 1/3 cup cannabis butter

- 3 mashed bananas

- 3/4 cup cane sugar

- 1/3 cup packed brown sugar

- 1 tsp. baking soda

- 1 tsp. baking powder

- 1/2 tsp. table salt

- 1 egg

- 2 tbsp. flour

- 1 tbsp. butter

- 1/8 tsp. ground cinnamon

Directions:

- Bring the heat of your oven to 350 f. and lightly butter a 10-cup muffin tray. Get out a large mixing bowl and mix the 1.5 cups flour, baking soda, baking powder and salt. In a separate bowl, mix the mashed bananas, egg, cane sugar and 1/3 cup melted cannabis butter. Stir this mixture into the first mixture until just blended. Spread this batter evenly into the greased or buttered muffin cups. In another bowl, combine the brown sugar, cinnamon and 2 tbsp. Flour. Cut in 1 tbsp. Butter. Sprinkle this mixture over the muffin batter in the trays. Bake 18 - 20 minutes; allow cooling on a wire rack and enjoying.

- **Nutrition:** Calories: 210 Fat: 6g Fiber: 2.4 Carbs: 35g Protein: 1.7 g

Lemon Coconut Muffins

- Preparation Time: 10-15 minutes

- Cooking Time: 15-20 minutes

- Servings: 8-10

Ingredients:

- 1 1/4 cup almond flour

- 1 cup shredded unsweetened coconut

- 2 tbsp. coconut flour

- 1/2 tsp. baking soda

- 1/2 tsp. baking powder

- 1/4 tsp. salt

- 1/4 cup of honey (raw)

- Juice and zest from 1 lemon

- 1/4 cup full-fat coconut milk

- 3 eggs, whisked

- 3 tbsp. medicated coconut oil

- 1 tsp. vanilla extract

Directions:

- Bring the heat of your oven to 350 f. In a small bowl, mix all the wet ingredients together. In a medium bowl, combine all the dry ingredients. Now pour the wet ingredients into the dry ingredients bowl and stir into a batter. Let your batter sit for a few minutes then stir it again. Now grease a muffin tin and fill each about two-thirds of the way full. Pop it in the oven and bake for about 20 minutes. Test the doneness of the muffin by inserting a toothpick in the center, and if it comes out clean, that means you are good to go. Remove from oven, let cool for a cool minute and serve!

- **Nutrition:** Calories: 296 Fat: 7,5g Fiber: 3.2 Carbs: 50g Protein: 1.9g

Marijuana Oatmeal Bars

- Preparation Time: 15 minutes

- Cooking Time: 25-30 minutes

- Servings: 14-16

Ingredients:

- 1¼ cups old-fashioned rolled oats

- 1¼ cups all-purpose flour

- ½ cup finely chopped toasted walnuts (see Note)

- ½ cup of sugar

- ½ teaspoon baking soda

- ¼ teaspoon sal t

- 1 cup cannabutter, melted

- 2 teaspoons vanilla

- 1 cup good-quality jam

- 4 whole graham crackers (8 squares), crushed

- Whipped cream, for serving (optional)

Directions:

- Preheat the oven to 350°F. Grease a 9-inch square baking pan. In a bowl, put in and combine oatmeal, flour, walnuts, sugar, baking soda, and salt. In a small bowl, combine the butter and vanilla. Add the butter mixture to the oat mixture and mix until crumbly. Reserve 1 cup for topping, and press the remaining oat mixture into the bottom of the baking pan. Spread the jam evenly over the top. Add the crushed crackers to the reserved oat mixture and sprinkle over the jam. Bake it for around 25 to 30 minutes, or until the edges are browned. Cool completely in the pan on a rack. Cut into 16 squares. Serve, adding a dollop of whipped cream if desired. Storing it in a glass container in the fridge will help preserve it.

- **Nutrition:** Calories: 299 Fat: 6.8g Fiber: 4.1 Carbs: 67g Protein: 3.1

Jane's Chewy Pecan Bars

- Preparation Time: 20 minutes
- Cooking Time: 1 hr. and 15 minutes

Ingredients:

- Nonstick baking spray
- 2 cups plus
- 2 tablespoons all-purpose flour, divided
- ½ cup granulated sugar
- 2 tablespoons plus
- 2 tsp. cannabutter
- 3½ teaspoons unsalted butter, cut into pieces
- ¾ teaspoon plus kosher pinch salt, divided
- ¾ cup packed dark brown sugar
- 4 large eggs
- 2 teaspoons vanilla extract
- 1 cup light corn syrup
- 2 cups chopped pecans
- Pecan nuts cut in half

Directions:

- Preheat the oven to 340°F. Grease the pan using a nonstick spray and line with parchment paper with an overhang on two sides so you can easily lift the bars from the pan. (The filling is sticky and can make it hard to remove without the parchment.)

- By utilizing a blender or food processor, pulse flour, the sugar, kinds of butter, and ¾ teaspoon of salt until combined. The mixture will form into clumps. Transfer the dough to the prepared pan. Press it firmly and evenly in the bottom of the pan. Pierce the crust all over with a fork and bake until light to a medium golden brown, 30 to 35 minutes.

- Using the same food processor bowl, combine the brown sugar, the remaining 2 tablespoons flour, pinch salt, eggs, vanilla, and corn syrup. (Add the corn syrup last, so it doesn't get stuck on the bottom of the food processor.) Pulse until completely combined. Turn the mixture into a large bowl and add the pecans. Spoon the pecan mixture evenly over the baked crust. Place a few extra pecan halves on the top of the filling as decoration.

- Place the pan back into the oven and let it bake until the center is just set 35 to 40 minutes. On the off chance that the inside still wiggles, prepare for a couple of more minutes; if you notice the bars are beginning to puff in the center, remove them right away. Put them in a rack and leave to cool before cutting into 16 (2-inch) squares and lifting the bars out.

- Storage: Keep the bars in an airtight container at room temperature for 3 to 5 days or freeze for up to 6 months. They can be very sticky, so wrap them in parchment or wax paper.

- **Nutrition:** Calories: 190 Fat: 1.5g Fiber: 4.1 Carbs: 26g Protein: 1g

Orange Creamsicle Cookies

- Preparation Time: 10 minutes

- Cooking Time: 10-15 minutes

- Servings: 24 pcs

Ingredients:

- 14 tablespoons (1¾ sticks) unsalted butter, softened

- 2 tablespoons cannabutter, softened

- ½ cup granulated sugar

- ½ cup packed light brown sugar

- 1 large egg, at room temperature

- 1½ tablespoons orange juice

- 2¼ cups all-purpose flour

- 2 tablespoons grated orange zest

- 1 teaspoon baking soda

- ½ teaspoon salt

- 2 cups white chocolate chips

Directions:

- Preheat the oven to 340°F. Put parchment paper on the baking sheet. By utilizing an electric mixer or stand mixer on medium speed, beat the kinds of butter and both sugars together for about 2 minutes. Add the egg and orange juice and mix for 30 seconds. Add the flour, zest, baking soda, and salt, and mix on low speed, increasing to medium-low speed, until the dough comes together. Stir in the chocolate chips until incorporated. Drop heaping 2-tablespoon scoops of the dough 2 inches apart onto the prepared baking sheets. Bake the cookies until lightly golden, which may take about 8 to 10 minutes. Let cool for 3 minutes on the baking sheet, and then transfer the cookies to a wire rack to finish cooling.

- Storage: Keep the cookies in an airtight container for 4 to 5 days or freeze for up to 6 months.

- **Nutrition:** Calories: 275 Fat: 2g Fiber: 4.1 Carbs: 26.4g Protein: 1.6g

Blueberry Muffins

Time: 35 minutes plus cooling time

Serving size: 6 muffins
Prep time: 10 minutes
Cook Time: 25 minutes

Ingredients:
- ½ cup frozen or fresh blueberries
- 1 cup all-purpose flour
- 1 teaspoon baking powder
- ⅛ teaspoon salt
- ½ teaspoon vanilla extract
- 1 egg
- ½ cup of sugar
- ¼ cup milk
- ⅛ cup unsalted butter
- ¾ cup cannabis-infused butter

Equipment:
- Large mixing bowl
- Muffin pan
- Non-stick baking spray
- Cooling rack

Directions:
1. Set your oven to 375° F and let it preheat while you make the muffin batter.

2. Spray the cups of your muffin pan with non-stick spray and set it aside.

3. In a large mixing bowl, combine the baking powder, salt, and flour and mix well.

4. Create a well in the center of the flour mixture and cut the cannabis butter up into blocks, dropping them into the well. Use your fingers to rub the butter into the flour to form crumbs.

5. Add the sugar and mix well.

6. Crack the eggs into the mixture and beat until you achieve a creamy texture.

7. Slowly add the milk and vanilla extract and mix well until combined. Do not over-mix.

8. Fold the blueberries gently into the batter until evenly distributed throughout.

9. Spoon or ladle the batter into the cups of the muffin pan, filling a maximum of 2/3 of each cup. Start by filling ½ of each cup until all cups are half-filled. Afterward, go back and add to each cup until all 12 cups are evenly filled with batter.

10. Pop the muffin pan into the oven and bake for 20 to 25 minutes, or until the muffins have risen and an inserted toothpick comes out clean.

11. Remove from the oven when done, turn out onto a cooling rack, and allow the muffins to cool.

12. Store in the fridge in a Ziploc bag for a grab-and-go-breakfast or snack or keep in the freezer for a later date.

Salted Caramel Popcorn

Time: 25 minutes
Serving size: 2 servings of 3 cups each
Prep time: 10 minutes
Cook Time: 15 minutes

Ingredients:
- 6 cups of popped popcorn, plain
- ½ ounce of cannabutter
- 1/8 cup regular butter
- ½ cup dark brown sugar
- 1/8 cup honey
- 1 teaspoon sea salt (regular table salt will also do the trick)
- 1/3 teaspoon baking soda
- ½ teaspoon of either vanilla or maple extract

Equipment:
- 2 large baking sheets
- Parchment paper (optional)
- Medium-sized saucepan
- Candy thermometer (optional)
- Large bowl

Directions:
1. Switch on your oven to 225° F and let it preheat while you prep your popcorn.

2. Pop your popcorn using an air fryer, a regular popcorn maker, a microwave, or a pot on the stovetop. Once you have popped your corn, set it aside in a large bowl.

3. Grease or line your baking sheets. You can use parchment paper to line them or you can grease them with butter. Be sure to use a generous amount of butter if you are choosing to grease the trays. Set the lined or greased trays aside.

4. Set your stovetop to medium heat and melt the cannabis butter in the saucepan.

5. Once the cannabutter is melted, add the brown sugar, honey, and ¼ teaspoon of the salt. Stir until all the ingredients are dissolved and then continue to cook the mixture until it reaches a boil, stirring regularly.

6. When the mixture comes to a boil, reduce the heat to a simmer. If you have a candy thermometer

handy, you can use this to tell when the caramel mix reaches a temperature of 250° F. If you don't have a candy thermometer, don't fret — you can get quite close to the right temperature by letting the mixture cook at a simmer for about 1 ½ minutes.

7. When the caramel mixture is ready, remove the saucepan from the heat and stir in the baking soda and your choice of extract. Add these ingredients quickly and stir, the mixture will turn a light brown color and become frothy.

8. It is important to work quickly at this point in the cooking process because the caramel will start to cool and harden.

9. Quickly pour the caramel over the popcorn you set aside earlier. Toss the popcorn in the caramel or stir the mixture through thoroughly until the popcorn is completely and evenly coated.

10. Spread your coated popcorn out on the baking sheets. Ensure that each baking sheet only has a single layer of evenly spread popcorn.
11. Sprinkle the coated popcorn with the remaining salt.
12. Place the baking sheets into the oven and bake the popcorn for 15 minutes.
13. After 15 minutes, remove the baking sheets from the oven and break the popcorn mixture up into pieces by giving it a good stir.
14. Place the baking sheets back in the oven and let the mix bake for a further 15 minutes.
15. Once done, remove the baking sheets from the oven and allow your salted caramel popcorn to cool. To store the balance, place it in an airtight container once it has completely cooled down.

Chocolate Chex

Time: 20 minutes
Serving size: 3 cups of chocolate Chex (serving size suggestion: ¼ to ½ cup of cereal)
Prep time: 5 minutes
Cook Time: 15 minutes

Ingredients:
- 3 cups of Chex cereal
- 1/3 cup of chocolate chips, semi-sweet or milk chocolate
- 1/6 cup of cannabis peanut butter (please refer to the recipe in this book for instructions)
- 2/3 ounce butter
- 1 teaspoon of vanilla extract
- ½ cup of powdered sugar

Equipment:
- Large mixing bowl
- Medium saucepan
- Plastic bag

Directions:
1. Place the Chex cereal into a large mixing bowl and set it aside.

2. Set your stove to medium heat and place the butter, cannabis peanut butter, and chocolate chips into a medium-sized saucepan over the heat. Allow all the ingredients to melt completely, stirring to combine and prevent burning.

3. Remove the saucepan from the heat and pour the chocolate and peanut butter mixture over the Chex

cereal in the mixing bowl.

4. Stir the cereal and chocolate to mix well until the cereal is thoroughly and evenly coated. Be sure to stir gently so that you don't crush the cereal in the process.

5. Allow the mixture to stand and cool down for a few minutes until it begins to set. Pour the coated cereal and powdered sugar into a non-scented plastic bag and shake well to coat the cereal with the powdered sugar.

6. Open the bag and spread the chocolate-coated cereal out in an even layer and allow to set completely.

7. Store in an airtight container for a quick grab-and-go snack.

Popcorn Bars

Time: 30 minutes plus cooling time
Serving size: 3 to 4 popcorn bars
Prep time: 10 minutes
Cook Time: 20 minutes

Ingredients:
- 2 tablespoons of cannabis butter
- 1 ½ cups of regular marshmallows or miniature marshmallows
- 1 ¼ tablespoons of peanut butter
- 2 cups of popped plain or caramel popcorn
- ¼ cup peanuts
- ¼ cup miniature chocolate chips

Topping Ingredients:
- 1/8 cup miniature marshmallows or regular marshmallows cut up
- 1/8 cup of miniature chocolate chips

Equipment:
- Small baking pan or dish
- Parchment paper (optional)
- Non-stick cooking spray (optional)
- Saucepan

Directions:
1. Set your oven to 350° F and allow it to heat up while you're preparing your popcorn bars.

2. Line the bottom of your baking pan or dish with parchment paper or, alternatively, spray it with non-stick cooking spray.

3. Set a saucepan over medium heat and melt the cannabis butter.

4. Once the cannabutter is melted, stir in the marshmallows and continue stirring until the marshmallows have all completely melted and mixed well with the butter. Add the peanut butter and stir well again to combine the ingredients.

5. Pour the popcorn into the marshmallow mix and stir to thoroughly and evenly coat all the popcorn.

6. Spoon half of the coated popcorn into your baking dish and compress it into a layer by pressing down on it with your hands.

7. Sprinkle the peanuts and chocolate chips on top of the layer of marshmallow and popcorn mix.

8. Spoon the rest of the popcorn on top and press down to form a compact layer.

9. Sprinkle the topping marshmallows and chocolate chips over the top and bake the bars for five to seven minutes.

10. Remove from the oven and allow it to cool completely. Chill the bars in the fridge before cutting them up. Store leftovers in an airtight container.

Peanut Butter Fudge

Time: 15 minutes plus cooling time
Serving size: 64 1-inch by 1-inch pieces of peanut butter fudge
Prep time: 5 minutes
Cook Time: 10 minutes

Ingredients:
- 1 cup of peanut butter, smooth
- 1 cup of cannabis butter, preferably unsalted to minimize sodium
- ¼ teaspoon salt
- 1 teaspoon vanilla extract
- 1 lb. powdered sugar

Equipment:
- Microwave-safe mixing bowl
- 8-inch by 8-inch pan
- Tin foil or wax paper
- Non-stick cooking spray
- Handheld mixer (optional)

Directions:
1. Line your pan with either parchment paper or tin foil, ensuring to line the sides as well as the bottom, and then spray with non-stick spray. Set aside.

2. Into the microwaveable bowl, add the cannabis butter, salt, and peanut butter. Microwave on medium heat until all the ingredients have melted. Stir regularly to prevent burning and combine ingredients as they melt.

3. Once melted, add in the vanilla extract and the powdered sugar and stir to incorporate. If you have a hand mixer, you can create a lighter texture by whipping it up for a couple of minutes.

4. Pour the fudge mixture into your prepared pan and smooth the top off with a spatula or a spoon.

5. Cover the pan and place in the fridge until the fudge has set.

6. Once the fudge has set, remove the pan from the fridge and cut the mixture up into blocks of 1-inch by 1-inch. Store in an airtight container in the fridge for up to one week.

Classic Chocolate Brownies

Time: 45 minutes plus cooling time
Serving size: 16 classic cannabis brownies
Prep time: 15 minutes

Cook Time: 30 minutes

Ingredients:
- ½ cup cannabis butter
- 1 cup white sugar (you may substitute brown sugar if desired)
- 2 eggs
- ½ cup all-purpose flour
- 1/3 cup unsweetened cocoa powder
- 1 teaspoon vanilla extract
- ¼ teaspoon salt
- ¼ teaspoon baking powder
- 3 mint leaves, minced (optional – mint helps to offset the cannabis flavor in the brownie batter)

Frosting (Optional):
- 3 tablespoons cannabis butter, softened
- 1 tablespoon honey
- 1 cup of confectioner's sugar
- 1 tablespoon vanilla extract

Equipment:
- Non-stick cooking spray
- 8-inch baking pan or heat-proof oven dish
- Large saucepan
- Hand mixer (optional)
- Mixing bowls
- spatula

Directions:
1. Preheat your oven by setting it to 350° F and let it heat up while you prepare the brownie batter.

2. Grease an 8-inch square oven pan or dish with non-stick cooking spray and set it aside.

3. Set your stove to medium heat and place a large saucepan with the cannabis butter in it over the heat to melt the butter.

4. Once the cannabis butter has completely melted, remove the saucepan from the heat, add the sugar, eggs, and vanilla extract, and stir in thoroughly.

5. Add the salt, unsweetened cocoa powder, flour, baking powder, and optional minced mint leaves and beat the batter until smooth and well combined. If you have a hand mixer, you may want to use it to beat the batter at this point.

6. Pour the brownie batter into your prepared baking pan or oven dish and smooth it out evenly with a spoon or a spatula.

7. Place the dish of batter in the center of the preheated oven and bake for 25 to 30 minutes. Be careful not to overcook the brownies.

8. Once baked, remove the brownies from the oven and allow them to cool on a countertop for at least five minutes before cutting. Allowing them to cool to room temperature is preferable to avoid crumbling while cutting. Freshly baked goods are more prone to crumbling the warmer they are when you slice them.

9. Cut into squares and store the balance in an airtight container or freeze for a convenient and easy-to-grab snack on the go.

Frosting (optional):
1. Combine all of the ingredients in a mixing bowl until well combined and the frosting is smooth.

2. Frost the brownies while they are still warm so that the frosting melts slightly into gooey frosted brownie goodness.

Canna Coffee and Tea

Coffee has become a mighty industry, with popular brands and outlets each offering that something special to get you hooked and keep you coming back for more. You can be your own brewmaster right at home by adding a canna-caffeine boost to your favorite coffee. Three simple ways of making cannabis-infused coffee include:
- Adding cannabis-infused milk instead of regular milk
- Adding a cannabis tincture to your cup
- Using cannabis-infused sugar in place of regular sugar

Time: 10 minutes
Serving Size: 1 cup of coffee
Prep Time: 5 minutes
Cook Time: 5 minutes

Ingredients:
- 1 cup of coffee or tea, slightly cooled
- Canna milk/sugar/tincture

Directions:
Making a basic cup of cannabis coffee or tea is really simple. You just brew your tea or coffee as usual and either add a few drops of the tincture to your cup or replace your regular milk or sugar with the cannabis-infused version. We have easy recipes to follow in Chapter 2 that will guide you through making your own cannabis infusions for your edibles.

Iced Canna Coffee

Time: 5 minutes
Serving Size: 1 to 2 servings
Prep Time: 2 minutes
Cook Time: 3 minutes

Ingredients:
- 1/2 cup warm water
- 5 ounces sweetened condensed milk
- 2 teaspoons instant coffee granules
- 1/2 cup cannabis-infused milk
- 1 tablespoon chocolate syrup
- 12 ice cubes

Equipment:
- Blender
- Small bowl

Directions:

1. In a small bowl, dissolve the coffee in the water.

2. Pour the coffee into the blender and add all the other ingredients. Flip the 'on' switch and blend until your iced coffee has the ideal consistency.

Tip: You can keep some of the ice cubes aside and add them to the cup before pouring in the iced coffee.

Note: If you don't normally have cannabis milk at hand, you can substitute regular milk and add your canna kick in the form of a few drops of tincture instead.

Chocolate Olive Oil Cake

Preparation Time: 15 minutes

Cooking Time: 30 minutes

Servings: 6-8

Ingredients:

- 3 cups all-purpose flour
- 2 cups of sugar
- 6 tablespoons good-quality cocoa powder
- 2 teaspoons baking soda
- 1 teaspoon salt
- ½ cup finely chopped nuts or dried fruit (optional)
- ¾ cup canna oil
- 2 tablespoons white vinegar
- 1tablespoon vanilla
- 2 cups cold water Powdered sugar, for dusting

Directions:

1. Preheat the oven to 350°F. Grease and flour two 8-inch cake pans or lines a 12-cup muffin tin with muffin liners. In a bowl, put in sugar and flour, cocoa powder, baking soda, salt, and nuts or dried fruit (if using). Whisk to incorporate. In another bowl, whisk together the oil, vinegar, vanilla, and water, then add to the flour mixture. With a hand mixer on medium-low speed, mix just until smooth. Pour into the prepared cake pans or muffin tin. Bake 30 to 40 minutes for cake or 20 to 25 minutes for muffins, or until a toothpick inserted in the center comes out clean (start checking early to avoid over baking). Cool completely. Before serving, dust with powdered sugar.

Nutrition:

Calories: 210 Fat: 6.8g Fiber: 4.1 Carbs: 34.6g Protein: 2.1g

Orange Almond Cake

Preparation Time: 15 minutes

Cooking Time: 45-50 minutes

Servings: 6-8

Ingredients:

- 2 cups packed almond flour, plus more for dusting
- 1 teaspoon baking powder
- ½ teaspoon baking soda
- 1 teaspoon ground cinnamon
- 1 teaspoon ground ginger
- ½ teaspoon salt
- 3 eggs, lightly beaten⅔ cup honey plus1 teaspoon, divided
- ¼ cup canna oil
- Zest and juice (¼ cup) of 1 orange
- 1 cup fresh raspberries

Whipped cream, chopped toasted almonds or pistachios, and powdered sugar, for garnis**Directions:**

1. Preheat the oven to 325°F. Grease a 9-inch spring form pan and dust the inside with almond flour. In a large bowl, whisk together the almond flour, baking powder, baking soda, cinnamon, ginger, and salt. In another bowl, whisk together the eggs, ⅔ cup of the honey, oil, and orange zest. The dry ingredients will then be added to the egg mixture and fold in until just a few lumps remain, then gently fold in the raspberries. Put the mixture in the prepared pan and smoothen the top part. Bake for 45 to 50 minutes, or until the edges are browned, and the center is set. Warm the remaining 1 teaspoon honey with the orange juice. Brush this onto the warm cake—it'll sink right in—then let it cool completely in the pan. To serve, garnish slices with whipped cream, chopped almonds or pistachios, and a dusting of powdered sugar.

Nutrition:

Calories: 219 Fat: 5.8g Fiber: 6.4 Carbs: 32.1g Protein: 3.2g

Chocolate-Covered Pretzels

Time: 30 minutes
Serving size: Yields as many chocolate-covered pretzels as there are in a bag
Prep time: 10 minutes
Cook Time: 20 minutes

Ingredients:
- 1 bag of pretzels
- 3 tablespoons powdered sugar
- ¼ cup cannabis butter
- 3 tablespoons cocoa powder

Equipment:
- Double boiler
- Baking sheet
- Wax paper

Directions:
1. Using the double boiler, melt the cannabutter.

2. When the cannabis butter is completely melted, use a sieve to add the powdered sugar and cocoa powder. A sieve will get rid of clumps and aerate the dry ingredients.

3. Over low heat, stir the mixture until all the ingredients have been well incorporated and a smooth texture is achieved.

4. Once smooth and combined, switch off the heat but leave the double boiler on the stovetop.

5. Line a baking sheet with wax paper and set it down next to the stove.

6. Using a fork, add the pretzels to the chocolate sauce mixture one at a time, dipping them in and removing them with the fork. Shake each pretzel lightly to remove excess chocolate sauce.

7. Place the pretzels on the lined baking sheet as you finish coating each one.

8. Place the baking sheet in the fridge and chill the pretzels until set.

9. Store in an airtight container.

S'mores Cannabis Brownies

Time: 45 minutes
Serving size: 10 s'mores brownie squares
Prep time: 10 minutes
Cook Time: 35 minutes

Ingredients:
- ¼ cup of cannabis butter, melted
- ¼ cup of either sunflower oil or a light vegetable oil
- 1 cup brown sugar
- 1 teaspoon vanilla extract
- ½ cup all-purpose flour or whole wheat flour
- ¼ teaspoon sea salt
- 1/3 teaspoon baking powder
- 1/3 cup unsweetened cocoa powder
- 1 cup miniature marshmallows
- 4 graham crackers
- 8 ounces of milk chocolate

Equipment:
- Deep medium-sized baking pan or dish
- Parchment paper
- Large mixing bowl
- Whisk

Directions:
1. Set the heat of your oven to 350° F and let it heat up while you prepare the brownies.

2. Line a deep medium-sized baking dish with a piece of parchment paper.

3. Whisk the eggs, sea salt, vanilla extract, brown sugar, and baking powder in a mixing bowl until the ingredients are well incorporated.

4. Add the flour and cocoa powder and mix again.

5. Add the melted cannabis butter and sunflower or light vegetable oil.

6. Pour the brownie mixture into the prepared baking dish or pan.

7. Place the dish in the oven and bake for approximately 15 minutes.

8. While you are waiting for the brownies to bake, crush the graham crackers and chop up the milk chocolate.

9. Add the broken-up graham crackers, miniature marshmallows, and milk chocolate to a mixing bowl.

10. Once the 15 minutes is up and the brownies are done baking, remove the baking dish from the oven and sprinkle the graham cracker, mini marshmallow, and chocolate mixture over the top.

11. Place the baking dish back into the oven and bake for another 15 to 20 minutes or until an inserted toothpick or skewer comes out clean.

12. Remove from the oven and place on a countertop to cool before cutting. Cut the baked brownie mix into 10 squares.

Peanut Brittle

Time: 45 minutes
Serving size: 10 servings of broken-up peanut brittle
Prep time: 15 minutes
Cook Time: 30 minutes

Ingredients:
- ½ a cup of cannabis sugar
- 1 tablespoon regular butter (cannabis butter may be substituted for a more potent peanut brittle, depending on your preference)
- ¼ teaspoon sea salt
- ½ a cup of peanuts, shelled

Equipment:
- Jelly roll pan
- Saucepan
- Parchment paper

Directions:
1. Use parchment paper to line the jelly roll pan and then set it aside.

2. Place the saucepan over medium heat and add the butter, or cannabis butter if you are substituting. Melt the butter completely.

3. Add the sea salt and cannabis sugar to the melted butter and stir until the dry ingredients are entirely dissolved.

4. Once dissolved, remove the saucepan from the heat and add in the shelled peanuts. Mix well to evenly and thoroughly coat all the peanuts without too much clumping together.

5. Quickly pour the peanut brittle mixture into the lined jelly roll pan and use a spoon or spatula to

spread the mixture into an even layer.

6. Place the pan into the fridge and chill for 30 minutes or until set and brittle.

7. Remove the brittle from the pan, peel off the parchment paper, being careful not to leave any paper behind in the brittle, and break up the brittle by smashing it with a rolling pin or other heavy object.

8. Divide the brittle up into 10 equal amounts, place each portion into a sealable bag and store.

Marshmallows

Time: 50 minutes plus cooling time

Serving size: 18 servings
Prep time: 20 minutes
Cook Time: 30 minutes

Ingredients:
- 1 cup of confectioner's sugar
- 2 cups of cannabis sugar
- 1 tablespoon of light corn syrup
- 1 ¼ cups water
- 4 tablespoons gelatin, unflavored
- 2 egg whites
- 1 teaspoon vanilla extract

Equipment:
- 9-inch by 9-inch dish or pan
- Saucepans
- Bowls
- Candy thermometer
- Hand mixer or standing mixer

Directions:
1. Generously dust your dish or pan with confectioner's sugar

2. Set your stovetop to medium-high heat and place a saucepan over the heat with the cannabis sugar, corn syrup, and ¾ cup of the water in it. Stir well and allow the mixture to heat up until it reaches a temperature of between 250° and 265° F. You can use a candy thermometer to check the temperature or, if you don't have one, you can check that the syrup is ready when a small dollop dropped into some cold water becomes a solid ball.

3. While the syrup is cooking, create a double boiler with a deep saucepan or small pot and a bowl that fits over it. Bring some water to a simmer in the saucepan or pot. Place the bowl over the simmering water, without it touching the water, with the remaining water from the recipe in it and sprinkle the gelatin on top of the water. Let the bowl sit over the simmering water until the gelatin has completely dissolved, then set it aside in a warm place until the syrup has reached the desired temperature.

4. Once the syrup mixture has reached the right temperature, add the gelatin mixture to it and whisk

well. Set the syrup and gelatin aside again.

5. In another bowl, whisk the egg whites until they form soft peaks. A hand mixer or a stand mixer is ideal for this, as using a whisk requires a lot of arm power and stamina.

6. While continuing to beat the egg whites, start pouring the gelatin and syrup mixture into the whites. Pour slowly so that the syrup is poured in as a thin stream of liquid. The egg whites will become very stiff; this is when you add the vanilla extract.

7. Pour the marshmallow mix into the dish or pan that you prepared and let it set for around 8 hours before cutting into squares.

8. Store the balance in an airtight container in the fridge for an easy snack.

Pop Tarts

Time: 45 minutes
Serving size: 10 pop tarts
Prep time: 20 minutes
Cook Time: 25 minutes

Ingredients:
- 1 cup cannabis butter cut into cubes
- 2 cups all-purpose flour
- 1 tablespoon white sugar
- 1 teaspoon salt
- ¼ cup cold water
- ½ teaspoon vanilla extract
- 1 jar or package of your preferred frosting

Filling Ingredients:
- ¼ cup softened cannabis butter
- 2 tablespoons ground cinnamon
- ¼ cup white sugar

Equipment:
- Baking sheets
- Parchment paper
- Mixing bowls
- Blunt knife
- Plastic wrap

Directions:
1. Start by making the pop tarts themselves before the filling.

2. In a mixing bowl, add the salt, 1 tablespoon of the white sugar, and the flour. Mix the ingredients together.

3. Add the cannabis butter and cut it into the flour mix with a blunt knife. You can also use your fingers to rub the butter in. The mix will take on a crumb-like appearance and texture.

4. Mix in the vanilla extract and then add in the cold water slowly, one tablespoon at a time, mixing continuously. The dough will start sticking together until you can shape it into a ball.

5. Divide your dough into two equal quantities for better chilling and wrap each portion of dough in plastic wrap. Refrigerate the dough for at least an hour, if not longer.

6. While the dough is chilling, make the filling by whipping together all the filling ingredients in a mixing bowl. Set them aside until the dough has chilled.

7. Preheat your oven to 375° F.

8. While your oven is heating up, prepare your baking sheets by lining them with parchment paper and then setting them aside while you make the pop tarts.

9. Once sufficiently chilled, remove the dough from the fridge and roll it out flat on a floured surface. Roll the dough to a thickness of ½-inch.

10. Cut the rolled-out dough into 10 evenly sized rectangles.
11. Spoon a tablespoon of filling onto one half of each rectangle. Fold the other half of the rectangle over the filling and press down on the edges with a fork to seal the filling inside of the dough pocket.
12. Use the fork to poke holes in the top of each pop tart.
13. Place the tarts on the baking sheets and place them in the oven to bake for 25 minutes or until golden brown in color.
14. Remove the pop tarts from the oven and allow them to cool for around 15 minutes before frosting and enjoying.
15. Store the balance in an airtight container for an easy-to-grab snack.

Rice Krispie Treats

Time: 20 minutes plus cooling time
Serving size: Dependent on the size of the bars
Prep time: 10 minutes
Cook Time: 10 minutes

Ingredients:
- ½ cup cannabis butter
- 5 cups cereal (Rice Krispies, Cocoa Pebbles, Fruity Pebbles, etc.)
- 4 cups miniature marshmallows or regular marshmallows cut up

Equipment:
- Large saucepan
- 13-inch by 9-inch baking pan or dish
- Spatula or wooden spoon
- Non-stick cooking spray (optional) or butter for greasing

Directions:
1. Grease your casserole dish with butter or non-stick cooking spray and set aside.

2. Place a large saucepan over medium to low heat and add in your cannabis butter. Allow the butter to melt completely but be careful not to let it burn.

3. Once the butter has melted, add in the miniature marshmallows and start stirring with that spatula or wooden spoon. Stir well as the marshmallows melt so that you evenly distribute the cannabis butter through the marshmallow mixture.

4. Once everything is melted, remove the saucepan from the heat and add in your cereal of choice. This is where the stirring becomes harder work, but it's important to mix all the ingredients thoroughly so that everything is evenly coated.

5. Once everything is well combined, spoon the cereal mix into the prepared pan or dish. Spread it out in an even layer and then compress it by pressing down firmly with your fingers. You may want to grease your hands with some butter before pressing down on the mixture to avoid it sticking to your hands.

6. Chill the cereal treats in the fridge or allow to set at room temperature until completely set before slicing into bars.

7. Store the balance in an airtight container.

Candied Bacon

Time: 35 minutes
Serving size: 12 pieces of cannabis candied bacon
Prep time: 10 minutes
Cook Time: 25 minutes

Ingredients:
- 12 slices of thick-cut bacon of your choice
- 1/3 cup of brown sugar
- 1 ½ teaspoons chili powder
- ¼ teaspoon cayenne pepper
- 1 gram of average decarbed cannabis, ground up

Equipment:
- Baking sheet
- Mixing bowl

Directions:
1. Start with setting the temperature of your oven to 350° F and let it preheat while you prepare the bacon.

2. In a mixing bowl, combine the ground cannabis, brown sugar, chili powder, and cayenne pepper and mix together well.

3. Evenly coat both sides of each slice of bacon with the cannabis-sugar mix before laying them on a baking sheet. Be sure to space the bacon slices evenly apart.

4. Sprinkle any leftover sugar mix over the top of the bacon.

5. Place the baking sheet in the center of your oven and bake for 25 minutes or until the bacon is caramelized and crisp. Flip the bacon pieces halfway through baking.

6. Store in an airtight container in the fridge for a day or so as an easy snack.

Chocolate Strawberries

Time: 30 minutes plus cooling time
Serving size: ½ lb. of chocolate covered strawberries
Prep time: 10 minutes
Cook Time: 20 minutes

Ingredients:
- 1 tablespoon cannabis olive oil
- ½ lb. fresh strawberries with their stems still attached
- 1/8 cup of white chocolate melting wafers
- 1 cup milk chocolate melting wafers

Equipment:
- Baking sheet
- Parchment paper
- Pot and mixing bowl to create a double boiler

Directions:
1. Line a baking sheet with parchment paper and set it aside.

2. Rinse off the strawberries, checking for imperfections or bugs, and pat them dry with a kitchen towel. Ensure that they are completely dry and set them aside.

3. Pour water into your base pot for your double boiler, place the pot over medium heat, and bring the water to a simmer.

4. Once the water is simmering, place your mixing bowl over the water but not touching it, and add your milk chocolate melting wafers. Melt the chocolate completely, stirring as it melts. Once melted, remove the chocolate from the heat.

5. Add your cannabis olive oil to the chocolate and stir in thoroughly. Ensure an even distribution of the oil through the chocolate so that each strawberry has the same potency.

6. Place the chocolate, strawberries, and prepared baking sheet next to each other for easy coating.

7. Holding the strawberries by their stems, dip each one into the infused melted milk chocolate, covering almost the whole strawberry. As you remove the strawberry from the chocolate, allow the excess chocolate to drip off back into the bowl. Lay each strawberry on the baking sheet, spacing them evenly apart.

8. Set the strawberries aside to set while you prepare the white chocolate.

9. Using a separate bowl, return to your double boiler with the white chocolate melting wafers and repeat the melting process as with the milk chocolate.

10. Once the white chocolate is completely melted, carefully place the bowl next to the baking sheet of setting strawberries. Use a spoon to drizzle the white chocolate generously and creatively over the milk chocolate covering the strawberries.

11. Store the balance in the fridge in an airtight container.

Cheeba Chocolate Chip Cookies

Cook Time: 10 minutes

If you love nuts in your cookies, try adding them with the chocolate chips!

Ingredients:

- ½ cup cannabutter, softened

- ½ cup real butter, softened

- 2 ¼ cups all-purpose flour

- 1 teaspoon baking soda

- ¾ cup brown sugar

- ¼ cup white sugar

- 2 eggs

- 1 teaspoon vanilla extract

- 2 cups semisweet chocolate chip s

Directions:

1. Heat oven to 350 degrees F. Spray 2 cookie sheets with nonstick spray.

2. With an electric mixer, mix cannabutter, butter, brown sugar, white sugar, baking soda, eggs and vanilla until combined. Add flour, mix until combined. Add chocolate chips, mix until combined.

3. Roll the dough by hand into 1 inch balls, and evenly place cookies 2 inches apart from each other onto the cookie sheets.

4. Bake 10 minutes.

5. Serve warm.

Pumpkin Pot Brownies

Ingredients:

- 2/3 cup packed brown sugar

- 1/2 cup canned pumpkin

- 1 whole egg

- 2 egg whites

- 1/4 cup cannabutter

- 1 cup all-purpose flour

- 1 teaspoon baking powder

- 1 teaspoon unsweetened cocoa powder

- 1/2 teaspoon ground cinnamon

- 1/2 teaspoon ground allspice

- 1/4 teaspoon salt

- 1/4 teaspoon ground nutme g

- 1/3 cup miniature semisweet chocolate pieces

Directions:
1. Preheat oven to 350 degrees F.
2. In a large mixing bowl, combine brown sugar, pumpkin, the whole egg, egg whites and oil.

3. Beat with an electric mixer on medium speed until blended.

4. Add flour, baking powder, cocoa powder, cinnamon, allspice, salt and nutmeg.

5. Beat on low speed until smooth. Stir in semisweet chocolate pieces.

6. Spray an 11×7 inch baking pan with nonstick coating.

7. Pour batter into pan. Spread evenly.

8. Bake 15 to 20 minutes or until a toothpick inserted near the center comes out clean.

Rocky Road Marijuana Brownies

Yield: 12 brownies
Ingredients:
- 1/2 cup cannabis-infused butter

- 1/8 cup butter

- 2 ounces unsweetened chocolate

- 4 ounces bittersweet or semisweet chocolate

- 3/4 cup all-purpose flou r

- 1/2 teaspoon salt

- 1 cup granulated sugar

- 2 large eggs

- 1 teaspoon vanilla extract

- 3/4 cup toasted almond slices

- 1 cup miniature marshmallows

Directions:
1. Preheat the oven to 350 degrees F. Line an 8-inch square baking pan with aluminum foil, and grease foil with either butter or vegetable shortening.
2. marijuana brownies, lining the pan

3. Melt the cannabutter, butter and chocolates over low heat in a medium saucepan stirring frequently. Set aside to cool for 5 minutes.

4. Stir together the flour and salt; set aside.

5. Stir the sugar into the melted cannabutter until well combined.

6. Beat in the eggs and vanilla and continue mixing until well incorporated.

7. Mix in the flour and salt until just incorporated.

8. Reserve 1/2 cup of the brownie batter, and spread the remainder into the prepared pan.

9. Bake batter in the pan for about 20 minutes. While it is baking, prepare the topping by stirring together the reserved batter with the toasted almonds and marshmallows .

10. After batter in pan has baked for 20 minute, remove from oven.

11. Spread topping over par-baked brownies and return to oven. Bake for about 10 more minutes or until marshmallows are browned and a toothpick inserted in the center comes out with just a few moist crumbs clinging to it.

12. Let cool in pan before using the foil to lift out the brownies and slice.

Honey Chocolate Brownies

Here is another recipe adapted to an all-honey version.

Ingredients:
- 1 cup melted marijuana butter or oil
- ½ cup melted unsweetened chocolate or cocoa powder
- 4 eggs
- 1 cup honey
- 2 teaspoons vanilla
- 2 cups unbleached white flour
- 2 teaspoons baking powder
- ½ teaspoon sea salt
- 1 cup raisin s
- 1 cup chopped nuts

Directions:
1. Preheat oven to 350 degrees F.
2. Whip the butter, chocolate, carob or cocoa and honey together until smooth. Add eggs and vanilla; mix well.

3. Add the dry ingredients, stir until dampened. Add the raisins and nuts and mix thoroughly.

4. Pour batter into a greased 9x13 inch baking pan. Bake for 45 minutes or until done.

5. Cut into 24 equal pieces (approximately 2" x 2"), each serving has 2 teaspoons of butter = high dose, or cut into 48 pieces (about 2" x 1") = medium dose.

Microwave Peanut Butter Swirl Brownie

Ingredients:
- 2 tablespoons cannabutter, softened

- 2 tablespoons sugar

- 1 1/2 tablespoons brown sugar

- 1 tablespoon cocoa powder

- 1 egg yolk

- 3 tablespoons flour

- Pinch of salt

- Splash of vanilla

- 1 tablespoon creamy peanut butter

Directions:
1. Mix the cannabutter, sugar, brown sugar, vanilla and egg yolk until smooth .
2. Stir in the salt and flour until well combined. Stir chocolate chips in last.

3. Pour into a ramekin or mug, then dot the top with peanut butter.

4. Swirl lightly with a butter knife.

5. Microwave for 45-75 seconds in the microwave until just done.

CannaCrack

Prep Time: 5 minutes
Cook Time: 15 minutes
CannaCrack is so good that you may need to check in to rehab!
Ingredients:
- 1/3 cup cannabutter

- 9 cups Chex cereal

- 1 cup semisweet chocolate chip s

- ½ cup peanut butter

- 1 teaspoon vanilla extract

- 1 ½ cups powdered sugar

Directions:

1. Place the cereal into a 1 gallon Ziplock freezer bag.

2. In a saucepan and on medium heat, add everything except the powdered sugar. Stir until melted and combined.

3. Pour the chocolate mixture onto the cereal inside the Ziplock bag. Seal the bag and shake it until all the cereal is coated with the chocolate mixture. Once the cereal is coated, pour the powdered sugar into the Ziplock bag, seal it, and shake it until the powdered sugar has coated everything.

4. Let cool, store in the same Ziplock bag, and eat with caution.

Oven-Baked Donut Holes

Time Required: 50 minutes
These donuts can be filled with your favorite pudding, jelly or sweet cream.
Ingredients:

- 1 cup white sugar

- ½ cup cannabutter, melted

- ¾ teaspoon ground nutmeg

- ½ cup milk

- 1 teaspoon baking powder

- 1 cup all purpose flour

- 1 teaspoon ground cinnamon

Directions :
1. Heat oven to 350 degrees F. Spray all of the cups of a mini-muffin pan with nonstick cooking spray.
2. With an electric stand mixer, mix ½ cup sugar, nutmeg, ¼ cup cannabutter, milk, baking powder and flour until combined

3. Fill mini-muffin cups ½ way full with donut mix. Bake 20 minutes.

4. When donuts are in oven, take 2 separate bowls and put ¼ cup melted cannabutter in one, and ½ cup sugar with cinnamon in the other.

5. When donuts have finished baking, remove them from the mini-muffin pan and, one-at-a-time, dip them first in the melted cannabutter followed by coating them with the cinnamon sugar.

6. Let cool.

Baked Backlava

Ingredients:
- 1 1/2 pounds walnuts, chopped

- 2 cups sugar

- 1/2 teaspoon nutmeg

- 3 teaspoons cinnamon

- 3 sticks canna butter

- 16 ounces phyllo dough

- 1 1/2 cups water

- 1 1/2 teaspoons Lemon Juic e

- 2 cups honey

- 1/2 teaspoon vanilla

Directions:

1. Preheat oven to 300 degrees F.

2. Set aside 2 tablespoons of the cannabutter. With the remaining butter, grease a 10×15 inch baking dish.

3. Take 10 sheets of phyllo dough, coat each with a good layer of butter and place them in the baking pan.

4. Mix together the walnuts with one cup of sugar, and pour this evenly into the pan over the phyllo dough sheets.

5. Take another five layers of phyllo dough, butter them and then place them in the pan as well. Bake the dough for 50 minutes.

6. While this is baking, take a saucepan and mix the leftover sugar with the spices, vanilla, water and lemon; cook until the mixture is syrupy. Add honey and heat for a minute. Remove from heat.

7. Cut the baklava into 2 by 2 inch squares or any other shape you want and then pour the syrup over them.

8. Now, have patience- set aside for two days so as to allow the honey to permeate. You are now ready for this spicy canna treat.

Butterscotch Canna-Pops

Ingredients:

- 1 cup sugar

- ½ cup cannabis corn syrup

- 2 tablespoons water

- 1 ½ teaspoons vinegar

- ¼ cup cannabutte r

- ¼ teaspoon vanilla extract

- Lollipop sticks

Directions:

1. Line baking sheet with waxed paper; set aside. Use cannabutter to grease the sides of the saucepan.

2. Combine the sugar, cannabis corn syrup, water and vinegar. Cook over medium-high heat for about 5 minutes to boiling, stirring constantly with a wooden spoon to dissolve the sugar. Continue to cook the mixture over medium heat, stirring constantly, while adding the butter (cut into 8 pieces), 2 pieces at a time.

3. The candy mixture should boil at a moderate, steady rate over the entire surface. Wait for a candy thermometer to read 300 degrees. This should take 25 to 30 minutes.

4. Remove the saucepan from the heat. Stir in the vanilla extract. Cool for 5 minutes.

5. Pour the mixture, 1 to 2 tablespoons at a time, onto the lined baking sheets. The mixture will make 2 to 3 inch circles.

6. Quickly place a lollipop stick into each piece of candy, twisting gently to cover with the candy mixture. Let the lollipops harden. Wrap the lollipops individually in clear plastic wrap to store at room temperature.

Cannabis Hard Candy

Ingredients:
- 1 cup cannabutter
- 2 cups white sugar
- ¾ cup water
- ¼ cup honey
- ½ cup corn or rice syrup
- ½ teaspoon sea salt
- 1 teaspoon vanilla or almond extract
- 2 tablespoons regular butter or coconut oi l

Directions:
1. Heat your honey and cannabutter to the point that they're in a liquid, pourable state. Set aside.
2. Use the regular butter or coconut oil to coat your candy molds.

3. Heat sugar, water and corn/rice syrup in a saucepan. Cover without stirring and bring to a boil.

4. Once the mixture is boiling, use a candy thermometer to check heat until the temperature reaches 132°C, the "soft-crack" stage. This should take about 15 minutes past the point of boiling.

5. Stir in cannabutter, salt and honey and continue heating until the mixture reaches 148°C. This is the "hard-crack" stage, and now the mixture should bubble to the edges of the pot.

6. Turn off the heat, wait for the bubbles to subside, and stir in the vanilla or almond extract.

7. Pour the mixture into the molds. If you're using lollipop sticks, place one end in the mold with the candy.

8. Allow the candy to cool for 30–60 minutes. Press the candy out of the molds afterwards.

9. Wrap the candy in aluminum foil or wax paper and refrigerate .

N.B. Remember that edibles can hit harder then you expect, so feel free to judge the amount of cannabis you use to make the butter according to your own experience.

Pina Co-Canna Pie Cake

Ingredients:
- 1½ cups Graham crackers, crumbled
- ½ cup cannabutter, softened
- 16 ounces (2- 8 ounce packages) cream cheese, softened
- ½ cup cream of coconut
- ½ cup Cool Whip
- ½ cup pineapple, crushed diced
- ½ cup cherries, dice d
- 1 cup coconut, shredded

Directions:
1. Mix graham cracker crumbs and softened cannabutter in a large bowl.
2. Transfer crust mixture to 9x13 inch baking pan. Press down firmly to cover surface of baking pan with Graham cracker mixture.

3. Beat cream cheese and cream of coconut together until smooth.

4. Add cool whip, pineapple and cherries. Fold ingredients together until evenly mixed.

5. Spread filling mixture on top of the Graham cracker crust. Top with shredded coconut.

6. Chill cake in refrigerator for 2 hours. Serve and enjoy.

Red-Hot White Fudge

Ingredients:
- 1 (14 oz) can sweetened condensed milk
- 12 ounce bag of white chocolate chips
- 2-4 ounce baking bars Ghirardelli white chocolate
- 2 jars red hot cinnamon candies (i.e. Red Hots or Cake Mate cinnamon decors)
- 12-14 drops cinnamon flavoring oil
- 2 tablespoons cannabis-infused coconut oil (melted)

Directions:
1. Line an 8×8 inch pan with wax paper, making sure that the wax paper covers all the way up the sides

of the pan.

2. Pour the sweetened condensed milk into a medium-size sauce pan.

3. Grab the white chocolate chips and break up the white chocolate bars; add them both to the condensed milk in your sauce pan.

4. Place the sauce pan over medium-low heat on your stove top, and melt the 3 ingredients together until the chocolate and milk are smooth.

5. Once the ingredients are creamy and smooth, add the 2 tablespoons of cannabis-infused coconut oil, and mix until the oil is fully combined with the chocolate. (The coconut oil will add a nice sheen to the fudge, too!)

6. After the coconut oil is combined, remove the sauce pan from the heat.

7. Stir in the 12-14 drops of cinnamon oil, tasting the chocolate afterwards and adjusting if you desire more spice. (Keep in mind you will also be adding the cinnamon candies) .

8. Add 1½ bottles of your cinnamon candies. (You will be using the remaining ½ bottle of candies to decorate the tops of your white fudge.)

9. Once the candies are mixed in, pour the white fudge batter into your prepped baking dish, spreading the fudge out with a spatula to ensure a smooth top and filled-in corners.

10. Place the remaining cinnamon candies on top of the fudge while trying to keep in mind how you will be slicing up the fudge. (I recommend standard rectangle pieces.)

11. Place the white fudge into the refrigerator, and chill the fudge for at least 2-3 hours or until firm.

12. Remove the white fudge from th e refrigerator, and carefully lift the sides of the wax paper to remove it from the pan. Carefully remove the wax paper from the fudge itself.

13. If you are giving the fudge as a gift, I suggest you cut off the edge pieces, as they will appear to be a little wrinkled in appearance. Nonetheless, they are still delicious!

14. Proceed to cut the cinnamon white fudge into pieces that fit your liking.

15. Serve immediately and enjoy! You can store the fudge pieces in the refrigerator for up to one week.

Cannabis Hard Candy and Lollipop

Ingredients:
- 1 cup sugar
- 1/3 cup corn syrup
- 1/2 cup water
- 1/4 teaspoon cream of tartar
- 1/4 to 1 teaspoon flavoring
- Liquid food coloring
- 1 to 2 teaspoon(s) citric acid (optional)

- 3 tablespoons cannabis tinctur e

Directions:
1. Prepare either a marble slab or an upside-down cookie sheet (air underneath the sheet will help the candy to cool faster) by covering it with parchment paper and spraying it with oil. If you're using molds, prepare the molds with lollipop sticks, spray with oil, and place them on a cookie sheet or marble slab.
2. In your pan, over medium heat, stir together the sugar, corn syrup, water and cream of tartar with a wooden spoon until the sugar crystals dissolve.

3. Continue to stir, using a pastry brush dampened with warm water to dissolve any sugar crystals clinging to the sides of the pan, then stop stirring as soon as the syrup starts to boil.

4. Place the candy thermometer in the pan, being careful not to let it touch the bottom or sides, and let the syrup boil without stirring until the thermometer just reaches 300 degrees F (hard-crack stage).

5. Remove the pan from the heat immediately, and let the syrup cool to about 275 degrees F before adding flavor, color, cannabis tincture and citric acid (adding it sooner causes most of the flavor to cook away) .

Caution

Be careful! The sugar syrup is extremely hot! If you burn yourself, run cold water over your hand for several minutes, but do not apply ice.
1. Working quickly, pour the syrup into the prepared molds and let cool for about 10 minutes. If you're not using molds, pour small (2-inch) circles onto the prepared marble slab or cookie sheet, and place a lollipop stick in each one, twisting the stick to be sure it's covered with candy.
2. Let the lollipops cool for at least 10 minutes, until they are hard. Wrap individually in plastic wrap or cellophane and seal with tape or twist ties.

3. Store in a cool, dry place.

Cannabis Toffee Candy

Ingredients:
- 2 cups roasted nuts (I like pecans)

- 1 cup sugar

- 1 cup butter (or cannabutter)

- 1 tablespoon light corn syrup

- 1/4 cup water

- 1 cup chocolate morsels

Directions:
1. Spread about 1 1/2 cups of chopped nuts on a non-stick baking sheet (may need to lightly grease it, but not too much) .
2. Bring sugar, butter and corn syrup to a boil over medium heat, stirring constantly to prevent burning.

3. Cook until the mixture reads about 300 to 310 degrees and mixture is golden brown (use candy thermometer and work fast; once it reaches 300, there isn't a lot of time until it burns).

4. Pour sugar mixture over chopped nuts on the baking sheet. Spread chocolate over hot candy and spread with a spoon (chocolate will start melting as soon as it hits the candy).

5. Sprinkle the rest of the nuts over the top of the chocolate, and let the sheet cool for about 30 mins or until the candy is cool.

6. The candy should break apart pretty easily after it has cooled.

Cannabis Peanut Butter Balls

Items Needed:
- Mixing bowl
- Double boiler
- Tray
- Wax paper
- Toothpicks

Ingredients:
- 1 1/2 cups peanut butter
- 1 cup cannabutter (hardened)
- 4 cups confectioners' suga r
- 1 1/3 cups Graham cracker crumbs
- 2 cups semisweet chocolate chips
- 1 tablespoon shortening

Directions:
1. Place the peanut butter and the cannabutter in a large mixing bowl. Slowly blend in the confectioners' sugar making sure that it does not get messy. Add Graham cracker crumbs and mix till consistency becomes solid enough to shape into balls. Make one-inch diameter balls.
2. Melt the chocolate chips and shortening in a double bottomed boiler. Prick a toothpick into each ball, and then dip them one by one in the chocolate mixture. Place the chocolate wrapped balls on wax paper on a tray. Place in the freezer for about 30 minutes until the balls are all solid.

3. This is an easy way to have a sweet snack and a cannabis kick at the same time. Just don't gobble them all down at once; go gradually, savor them, and relish them like you really want to. Share these awesome peanut butter balls with your friends, so that you all can feel the mellow kick coming on slowly, sweetly but surely!

Rice Krispie Treats

Ingredients:

- 1 bag miniature marshmallows (use fruit flavored marshmallows to change it up)
- 2 tablespoons unsalted butter (cannabis-infused butter)
- 2 tablespoons coconut oil (cannabis-infused coconut oil)
- 5 cups crispy rice cereal
- ¼ teaspoon almond extract (try a raspberry or strawberry with fruit flavored marshmallows)
- Note: You can choose to use both infused butter and coconut oil or just use one or the other.

Directions:

1. Spray bottom of cookie sheet with cooking spray (or parchment paper makes easier cleanup).
2. In pan over medium heat, melt butter, infused oil and extract together.

3. Continue heating over medium heat, and slowly add marshmallows to the mixture, stirring constantly to prevent scorching.

4. When the mixture is well-blended (remember don't overcook), remove from heat and immediately add cereal in small portions until the cereal is evenly covered. (Tip: Coat your spoon with a little oil first.)

5. Spread out onto cookie sheet, and press down with spoon into desired thickness.

6. Allow to cool and then cut into individual portions (15-20 servings).

7. Chocolate lovers can drizzle canna-shell chocolate across the top before cooling.

Caution

1. Too Much Caffeine Can Negatively Affect Your Experience:
2. If using chocolate in your recipe, please consider that caffeine is found naturally in cocoa beans, so any chocolate has a little bit of the stimulant. Candy bars generally have less than 10 milligrams, but the darker the chocolate, the higher the caffeine content.

Cannabis Apple Pie

Time Required: 2 Hours

Ingredients:

- 9-inch pie dish
- 2 sheets of refrigerated pie crusts
- 6 cups apples, cored, peeled, and sliced (Granny Smith, Golden Delicious, and/or HoneyCrisp)
- 1 tablespoon fresh lemon juice
- ⅓ cup brown sugar
- ½ cup granulated sugar

- ⅛ cup flour

- 1 teaspoon cinnamon, ground

- ½ teaspoon salt

- ⅛ teaspoon nutmeg, ground

- 1½ cups cannabutter, cube d

Directions :
1. Preheat oven to 375 degrees.
2. Press one pie crust sheet firmly into the bottom of the pie dish and up the sides of the pan.

3. Trim the edge of the dough with kitchen scissors; leave 1 inch of dough to hang over the edge of pan. Set aside.

4. Combine the apples and lemon juice in a large bowl. Mix well.

5. Add brown sugar, granulated sugar, flour, cinnamon, salt and nutmeg.

6. Mix well, making sure to coat all the apples.

7. Transfer the filling mix to the dough-lined pan.

8. Disperse cubed cannabutter on top of the apple filling evenly.

9. Place the second pie sheet over the filled pie. Trim edges appropriately, leaving 1 inch of dough hanging.

10. Fold the edge of the top layer of dough under the edge of the bottom layer of dough. Pinch dough sheets together to seal.

11. Cut an "x" across the top center of the dough to allow steam to escape.

12. Put the uncooked pie in the refrigerator to firm the dough (about 20 minutes).

13. Remove pie from refrigerator and bake the pie in the preheated oven for 1 hour, or until the crust is golden brown and the filling is bubbling.

14. Transfer pie to a wire rack and let cool to completely set for at least 1 hour before serving.

15. Serve with whipped canna-cream or cannabis ice cream for a heightened experience!

Cannabis-Infused Red Velvet Cake

Ingredients:
- 2 3/4 cups all purpose flour

- 1 3/4 cups sugar

- 1 teaspoon baking soda

- 2 teaspoons cocoa powder

- 2 large eggs, room temperature

- ¾ cannabis oil (coconut, canola…)

- ¾ cup canola oil

- 1 1/4 cup buttermilk

- 2 teaspoons red food colorin g

- 1 teaspoon vanilla

- 1 tablespoon white vinegar

  For Frosting:
- 16 ounces cream cheese

- 4 ounces cannabis butter, slightly softened

- 3 cups powdered sugar

- 2 teaspoons vanilla

Directions:

This cake is so very good; you will love having it in your repertoire. When you eat a slice that is medicated, be sure to save another sliver for later. It's one of those foods that you eat when you are stoned and want to just sit there eating it for the rest of your life. Fortunately, that feeling will pass, as it would not be a very productive, though delicious, experience.

1. Preheat oven to 325 degrees F.
2. Place parchment on the bottom of three 8-inch pans.

3. Mix all dry ingredients together. Beat eggs slightly. Add all wet ingredients together. Mix wet into dry ingredients.

4. Pour into prepared pans. Bake for 30 to 35 minutes.

5. When done, remove from oven and wait 5 minutes; then, turn out on cooling rack s

For Icing:

1. Place the butter in mixer and beat till soft. Add cream cheese and mix, stopping periodically to scrape bowl.
2. Beat till light colored; slowly add powdered sugar, waiting for it to be completely incorporated along with some air before adding more.

3. When all the sugar is incorporated, beat a few more minutes; add vanilla, beat and ice cake immediately.

Peanut Butter Ganja Goo Balls

N.B . The following recipe is made with an estimated amount of marijuana. Remember that edibles can hit harder than you expect, so feel free to judge the amounts according to your own experience. It is strongly advised to first learn how to calculate the strength of edibles.

Ingredients:

- 250 g melted cannabutter

- 225 g oats

- 250 g peanut butter (whether it is the smooth or chunky variant will be all up to you)

- 3 tablespoon honey

- 2 tablespoon ground cinnamo n

- 1-2 tablespoon cocoa powder

Directions:
1. Place all ingredients in one large bowl and stir until everything is mixed in.
2. Place the mix into the freezer and leave it for 10-20 minutes.

Mold the mixture into individual balls, to the size of your preference. After which, drop it onto some wax paper to set. Some people prefer adding other ingredients such as chopped walnuts, raisins, Rice Krispies or Corn Flakes, just to experiment.

1. More oats can be added if you find the end result a little too sticky and gooey, or add more honey or peanut butter if it turns out to be too dry. It is all about being creative and adding your own touch to this delicacy.
2. Once that is done, you are now ready to serve this scrumptious treat, which can be eaten for dessert, a snack, or just any time of the day you choose to have an edible. Enjoy!

Basic Recipe

Time: 3 to 4 hours
Serving Size: 1 cup of infused product
Prep Time: 10 minutes
Cook Time: 3 to 4 hours

Ingredients:
- 1 ¼ cup of your oil of choice/unsalted butter/honey/maple syrup/molasses OR 2 cups of milk
- ½ ounce of average decarboxylated cannabis

Equipment:
- 2 canning jars with a lids
- A 2- to 3-quart pot or saucepan
- A kitchen towel (not paper towel) to fold up and place at the bottom of the saucepan/pot. This will act as a buffer between your jar and the heat source.
- Cheesecloth/screen strainer/French press coffee pot

Directions:
1. Crumble the cannabis and place it in the first jar, along with the infusion medium of your choice. Swirl the jar around a few times to thoroughly combine the two ingredients.

2. Place the folded kitchen towel at the bottom of the pot and the jar on top of the towel.

3. Fill the pot with as much water as possible. The jar should not float but the water level should at least reach a little above the level of the oil inside the jar.

4. Place the pot on the stovetop over medium heat and allow the water to heat up to a simmer.

5. Keep an eye on the water level throughout the infusing process; don't let it drop too low below the level of the oil. Top the water up every now and then as it evaporates.

6. Open the lid of the jar approximately every 30 minutes to relieve any pressure that has built up

inside it and to give the oil mixture a little stir.

7. Allow the cannabis mixture to infuse for around 3 to 4 hours (1 hour for milk).

8. After infusing, allow the oil to cool a little bit before straining out the marijuana crumbs.

9. You can strain your cannabis oil by pouring it through a piece of cheesecloth or a small screen strainer with fine mesh. Alternatively, you can also try using a French press coffee maker to strain the bits and pieces from the oil as if you were making coffee.

10. After straining, pour your infusion into the second canning jar and store it in a cool, dry place.

Cannabis Alcohol Tincture

Time: 4 days
Serving Size: 1 cup of tincture
Prep Time: 5 minutes

Cook Time: 4 days

Ingredients:
* ½ ounce of average decarboxylated cannabis, crumbled
* 1 1/8 cups of high-proof, food-grade alcohol like Everclear (Alternatively, you can also use any other high-proof spirit you prefer. Using spirits will flavor your tincture with the taste of that particular spirit.)

Equipment:
* A canning jar of the right size with a tight-fitting lid
* Cheesecloth or a small screen strainer
* Small dark-colored glass bottle with a dropper lid

Directions:
1. Combine the cannabis and alcohol in the canning jar and give it a really good shake.

2. Store the concoction in a cool, dry place for four days.

3. Give the jar a good shake once a day during the infusion process.

4. After four days of steeping, strain the tincture to remove the cannabis and pour it into the glass bottle.

Note: When using tinctures in drinks, you should start with a lower dose – a few drops at a time – to test the potency. If desired, you can add more the next time until you discover the ideal amount of tincture for your preferred potency.

Cannabis Sugar

Canna-sugar might take some patience to make, but it is worth the effort for its versatility.
Note: You cannot make cannabis sugar with fat such as oil or butter. You need to use an alcohol tincture so that the alcohol can evaporate, leaving the infused sugar crystals behind.

Time: Approximately 2 days
Serving Size: 3 cups of infused sugar
Prep Time: 10 minutes

Cook Time: 2 days

Ingredients:
- 3 cups of granulated sugar
- 1 cup of cannabis alcohol tincture

Equipment:
- Large baking sheet
- Rubber spatula
- Canning jars with lids

Directions:
1. Spread the sugar evenly across the bottom of the baking sheet and pour the alcohol tincture over it.

2. Stir the mixture until the sugar is soaked through. The mix will look like wet sand.

3. Cover the baking sheet with cheesecloth or another breathable covering that will allow the alcohol to evaporate but keep debris from falling into your sugar.

4. Put the sheet in a dry, safe place and let the concoction air dry for at least 48 to 72 hours or until all the alcohol has evaporated.

5. Stir the sugar regularly to dry it evenly throughout.

6. When the alcohol has evaporated, break up any large crystals, pour your canna-sugar into a jar or other airtight container, and store in a cool, dry place.

Chicken Wings

Time: 50 minutes
Serving Size: 2 to 3 servings
Prep Time: 10 minutes
Cook Time: 40 minutes

Ingredients:
- 3 lbs of chicken wings
- 2 tablespoons vegetable oil
- 1 teaspoon freshly ground black pepper
- 1 teaspoon kosher salt
- 3/4 cup low-salt soy sauce
- 1/4 cup freshly squeezed lime juice
- 1/4 cup freshly squeezed orange juice
- 3 tablespoons white wine vinegar
- 1/4 cup ketchup
- ¼ cup hoisin sauce
- 1/4 cup coconut sugar

- 1/2 teaspoon powdered ginger
- 1/2 teaspoon garlic powder
- 2 tablespoons cannaoil
- 2 teaspoons chili powder

Equipment:
- 2 baking sheets
- Parchment paper
- Mixing bowls
- Medium saucepan

Directions:
1. Start off by turning your oven to 400° F to preheat it while you prepare the chicken wings.

2. Line the two baking sheets with parchment paper and set them aside.

3. Rinse the chicken wings and pat dry with some paper towel.

4. Cut off and discard the tips of the wings, then find the wing joint and separate each wing into two pieces.

5. Pour the vegetable oil into a mixing bowl and toss the chicken wings in the oil. Coat them thoroughly and then lay them on the baking sheets, evenly spaced.

6. Sprinkle the salt and pepper over the chicken. Place the baking sheets in the oven and bake for 15 minutes.

7. Remove the baking sheets from the oven and turn the chicken over. Pop the sheets back in the oven and bake for a further 15 minutes. If you have a meat thermometer, the reading should be 150° F when it is inserted into a wing.

8. While you're waiting for your wings to bake, it's time to make the sauce.

9. Whisk all of the remaining ingredients together in a saucepan over medium-low heat and cook until the sauce thickens. When the sauce is ready, it should be thick enough that it coats the back of a spoon.

10. Once cooked, transfer the chicken wings to a big mixing bowl and pour the sauce over them. Toss the wings in the sauce so that they are all evenly coated.

11. When serving, if there is any sauce leftover in the bowl, drizzle it over the chicken wings.

Dates Wrapped in Bacon

Time: 30 minutes
Serving Size: 8 bacon-wrapped dates
Prep Time: 20 minutes
Cook Time: 10 minutes

Ingredients:
- 2 teaspoons cannabis butter
- 4 strips bacon
- 8 pitted dates

- 8 toothpicks
- 1 tablespoon goat's cheese

Equipment:
- Small knife
- Mixing bowl
- Baking sheet
- Toothpicks

Directions:
1. Begin by turning the oven on to 325° F and let it heat up while you're preparing the wrapped dates.

2. Cut the strips of bacon in half crosswise.

3. Using a small knife, cut a slit into each date and pull it open with your fingers.

4. Mix the goat's cheese and cannabis butter well in a small bowl and distribute the butter-cheese mix between the 16 dates.

5. Press the mix into each date and then close it up again.

6. Wrap one slice of bacon around each cheese-and-butter-stuffed date and secure the bacon in place by skewering the date with a toothpick.

7. Arrange the bacon-wrapped dates on a baking sheet so that the seam where the bacon closes around the date is facing the bottom.

8. Bake for about 10 minutes or until the bacon is crispy.

Bruschetta With Basil Pesto

Time: 20 minutes
Serving Size: Dependent on the size of the ciabatta bread
Prep Time: 10 minutes
Cook Time: 10 minutes

Ingredients:
- 3 tablespoons of cannabis-infused olive oil
- 1 loaf ciabatta bread
- 3 ripe tomatoes

Equipment:
- Bread knife
- Baking sheet
- Pastry brush

Directions:
For the canna-pesto recipe, please refer to the recipe detailed in this book under sauces.
1. Turn on the oven to 350° F and let it heat up while you prepare the bruschetta.

2. Slice the ciabatta loaf into thick slices – about an inch thick should do.

3. Brush the top of each slice of bread with the cannaoil. Place the slices on a baking sheet and toast

them in the oven for three minutes or until they are golden brown.

4. Remove the bread slices from the oven and spread basil pesto on each slice, then top with some diced tomato.

5. Put the baking sheet with the slices on it back into the oven and bake them for another five minutes or until the tomatoes start showing signs of cooking.

6. Remove from the oven and serve warm.

Bacon-Wrapped Jalapeños

Time: 40 minutes
Serving Size: 30 jalapeño halves stuffed and wrapped in bacon
Prep Time: 15 minutes
Cook Time: 25 minutes

Ingredients:
- 15 fresh 3-inch long jalapeño peppers
- 8 ounces of cream cheese at room temperature
- 1½ cups of shredded white cheddar cheese
- 3 tablespoons of canna-sriracha sauce (recipe can be found in the sauces chapter)
- ¼ cup mayonnaise
- 4 teaspoons cannabis-infused sugar
- 1 teaspoon freshly cracked black pepper
- ½ teaspoons dried onion powder
- ½ teaspoon dried garlic powder
- 1 tablespoon kosher salt
- 15 slices of thin cut bacon

Equipment:
- Baking sheet
- Teaspoon
- Medium-sized mixing bowl
- 30 toothpicks
- Non-stick baking spray

Directions:
1. Turn your oven on to 400° F to preheat it while you're assembling the jalapeños.

2. Line a baking sheet with aluminum foil and spray it with some non-stick baking spray.

3. Slice each jalapeño lengthwise in half and use a teaspoon to scrape the seeds out of each half.

4. Place the remaining ingredients, except for the bacon, into a medium-sized bowl and mix well together until everything is incorporated.

5. Use the cream cheese mix to full each half of the jalapeños and set them aside.

6. Cut the bacon slices crosswise in half and wrap each jalapeño half in half a slice of bacon. Skewer the wrapped pepper halves with a toothpick to hold the bacon in place.

7. Lay the jalapeño peppers on the baking sheet, evenly spaced apart, and pop them into the oven to bake for around 20 to 25 minutes or until the bacon has browned and become crispy.

8. Once done, remove the baking sheet from the oven and set aside to cool for five minutes.

9. Carefully remove each toothpick, season the peppers with salt and pepper to taste, and serve hot.

Mac 'n' Cheese Bites

Time: 24 hours
Serving Size: Varies depending on size of balls
Prep Time: 30 minutes + overnight
Cook Time: 3o minutes

Ingredients:
- 1/2 lb of cooked elbow macaroni pasta
- 2 cups of shredded cheddar cheese
- 1 cups of shredded gruyère cheese
- ¼ cup of cannabis-infused butter
- ¼ cup of unsalted butter
- ½ teaspoon of black pepper
- 1 teaspoons of salt
- ¼ teaspoon of cayenne pepper
- 6 ounces bread crumbs
- ½ cup of flour
- 2 cups of milk
- Oil for frying

Egg Wash:
- 2 eggs
- 2 tablespoons of milk

Equipment:
- Saucepan
- Whisk
- Large mixing bowl
- Large tray
- Wax paper
- Shallow bowls

Directions:
1. Heat up a saucepan over medium heat and melt the unsalted butter and the cannabis butter.

2. Gradually add the flour and whisk. The mixture will form a crumb-like consistency or a paste.

3. Slowly add the milk and whisk with vigor. At first, the butter and flour mix will appear to make lumps but whisking will break up these lumps until the base sauce becomes smooth and starts to thicken.

4. Once the sauce thickens, remove it from the heat and slowly begin adding in the two kinds of cheese,

whisking as you do so. Add them a bit at a time and ensure that you allow each added batch to completely melt before adding the next lot.

5. The end result should be a creamy cheesy sauce. Add in the salt, pepper, and cayenne pepper and mix well.

6. Pour the cheesy sauce over the macaroni noodles and mix it all together in a large bowl.

7. Put the macaroni and cheese sauce into the fridge and chill it for about two hours. The concoction will thicken, which will make it easier to shape into balls.

8. Line a large tray with wax paper to prevent the macaroni balls from sticking.

9. Once chilled, remove the macaroni from the fridge and shape it into balls. Arrange the macaroni balls on the tray, spaced evenly.

10. Put the tray in the freezer and leave it there overnight.
11. Heat oil in a saucepan over high heat until it reaches a temperature of 350° F. While you're waiting for the oil to heat up, prepare the mac 'n' cheese balls to be fried.
12. Mix the egg wash by adding the eggs and two tablespoons of milk together in a shallow bowl and whisking till combined.
13. Have your bread crumbs handy in a separate shallow bowl.
14. Remove the frozen mac 'n' cheese balls from the freezer and place the tray on the counter. Dip each ball into the egg wash and then coat each evenly in bread crumbs.
15. Pop your macaroni balls into the hot oil, a couple at a time. While frying, turn them over to cook evenly. Frying should take around five minutes per batch; they should be heated through and the outsides should be golden brown.
16. Serve them hot with a dipping sauce such as the sriracha hot sauce listed under sauces.

Cauliflower Fire Bombs

Time: 50 minutes
Serving Size: Dependent on the size of the cauliflower head
Prep Time: 10 minutes
Cook Time: 40 minutes

Ingredients:
- ½ a head of cauliflower
- ¼ cup all-purpose flour
- ¼ cup of water
- ½ teaspoon dried garlic powder
- ¼ teaspoon pepper
- ¼ teaspoon salt
- ⅛ cup of cannabis butter
- ¼ cup cayenne pepper hot sauce (You may like to substitute the sriracha hot sauce in the sauces section which will add an additional canna kick or any other hot sauce you prefer.)

Equipment:
- Large mixing bowl

- Baking sheet
- Non-stick baking spray

Directions:

1. Turn your oven on to 425° F and let it warm up while you prepare the cauliflower bombs.

2. Break the head of cauliflower into florets.

3. Mix together the flour, salt and pepper, and garlic powder in a large mixing bowl.

4. Put the cauliflower florets into the flour mixture and toss them until they are evenly coated.

5. Coat a baking sheet with non-stick baking spray and place the cauliflower florets into the sheet, spacing them evenly apart.

6. Pop them in the oven and bake for about 20 minutes.

7. While the cauliflower is baking, mix together the hot sauce and the butter, which will make buffalo sauce.

8. Once baked, remove the cauliflower from the oven and allow to cool slightly.

9. Coat each floret in the buffalo sauce, put them back onto the baking sheet, and pop them back into the oven for another 20 minutes.

10. Serve hot with a dipping sauce and crudités on the side.

Sweet Potato Fries

Time: 35 minutes
Serving Size: 2 to 4 servings depending on the size of the sweet potatoes
Prep Time: 10 minutes
Cook Time: 25 minutes

Ingredients:
- 2 big sweet potatoes
- 3 tablespoons of your choice of cannabis-infused cooking oil
- 1/2 teaspoon each salt and black pepper
- 1/4 teaspoon paprika
- 1/4 teaspoon dried garlic powder

Equipment:
- Vegetable peeler
- Knife
- Baking sheet
- Mixing bowl
- Parchment paper

Directions:

1. Ensure that the oven rack is correctly positioned in the upper third of your oven before switching it on and preheating to 425° F.

2. Line a baking sheet with parchment paper and set aside.

3. While your oven is heating up, peel the sweet potatoes and cut them up into one-inch-thick strips or wedges that are approximately three inches long.

4. Put your sweet potato fries into a mixing bowl with the cannaoil and toss to coat them evenly. Sprinkle the paprika, pepper, and salt over the fries.

5. Lay the sweet potato fries on the baking sheet, spreading them out evenly. Ensure that you don't overcrowd the sheet by baking too many fries on a single sheet.

6. Pop the fries in the oven and bake for 18 to 20 minutes or until they are golden brown and tender. Allow them to cool down for a few minutes before serving them.

Guacamole

Guacamole is the perfect dip to pair with nacho chips when you want to satisfy your cravings or the munchies.

Time: 25 minutes

Serving Size: Serves 2
Prep Time: 10 minutes
Cook Time: 15 minutes

Ingredients:
*   1 avocado
*   Juice of ⅓ lime
*   ⅓ teaspoon salt (or to taste)
*   ¼ cup diced onion
*   1 tablespoons fresh cilantro
*   ¾ teaspoons carboxylated cannabis
*   ¾ plum or Roma tomatoes
*   ⅓ teaspoon minced garlic
*   ⅓ teaspoon cannabis oil
*   A pinch of ground cayenne pepper

Equipment:
*   A medium-sized mixing bowl

Directions:
1. Grind up the cannabis until it's fine, dice the tomatoes, and chop up the cilantro.

2. Peel, remove the pits, and smash up the avocados. You can leave the smashed avocados slightly chunky or you can use a blender to achieve a smooth consistency.

3. Put all of the ingredients into the bowl and mix it all up until it's well combined.

Spiced Nuts

Time: 40 minutes plus cooling time

Serving size: 3 cups of spicy nuts
Prep time: 10 minutes
Cook Time: 30 minutes

Ingredients:
- 1 cup pecans
- 1 cup walnuts
- 1 cup cashews
- 1 teaspoon ground cumin
- 2 tablespoons curry powder
- Pinch of cayenne
- ½ teaspoon ground cardamom
- Salt to taste
- 3 tablespoons of cannabis oil

Equipment:
- Baking sheet
- Mixing bowl
- Non-stick cooking spray

Directions:
1. Start off by switching your oven on to 300° F to preheat while you prepare the nuts.

2. Spray a baking sheet or two with non-stick spray and set aside.

3. Toss all the ingredients in a large mixing bowl, ensuring that all ingredients are well mixed and that all the nuts are evenly and well coated.

4. Spread out the coated nuts on one or two baking sheets. Don't overcrowd the baking sheet – spread the nuts out evenly, allowing spaces between them for a better result.

5. Bake them for 20 to 30 minutes, stirring them up and around regularly to turn and toast them evenly.

6. After baking, remove from the oven, let cool, and store in an airtight container.

Spicy Chickpeas

Time: 40 minutes plus cooling time
Serving size: 16 ounces of spiced chickpeas
Prep time: 10 minutes
Cook Time: 30 minutes

Ingredients:
- 1 16-ounce can chickpeas
- 2 tablespoon cannabis olive oil
- ¼ teaspoon ground cumin
- ¼ teaspoon ground ginger
- ¼ teaspoon paprika (smoked is preferable, but plain will do just fine)
- ¼ teaspoon salt

Equipment:
- Colander or strainer
- Large mixing bowl
- Baking sheet
- Non-stick cooking spray or parchment paper

Directions:
1. Before you prepare the chickpeas, set your oven to 375° F so that it can preheat.

2. Drain the chickpeas in a colander or strainer.

3. Using a large mixing bowl, mix together all the ingredients until the chickpeas are well and evenly coated.

4. Spray a baking sheet with non-stick spray or line it with parchment paper to prevent sticking.

5. Spread the coated nuts out on the baking sheet evenly and bake for 30 minutes or until the chickpeas start to crisp.

6. Allow to cool and store in an airtight container.

Savory Popcorn

Time: 15 minutes plus cooling time

Serving size: 1 serving
Prep time: 5 minutes
Cook Time: 10 minutes

Ingredients:
- 1/4 cup cannabis-infused butter
- 1/2 cup popcorn kernels
- 1/4 cup canola/vegetable oil
- Salt to taste

Equipment:
Large stockpot with a lid

Directions:
1. Over medium-high heat, warm oil in a large stockpot.

2. Drop two to three corn kernels in the oil and cover the pot. When the oil is hot enough, the kernels will pop. When the test kernels pop, add the rest of the corn kernels, spreading them evenly across the bottom of the pot.

3. Cover the pot and let the kernels pop.

4. Shake the pot gently to shift the kernels so that all of them have a chance to pop.

5. Popping should occur in rapid succession. When the popping slows to two or so seconds between pops, it's time to remove the pot from the heat.

6. Drop the cannabis butter into the pot and mix well to evenly coat the popcorn. Sprinkle with salt as

desired.

Potato Chips

Time: 25 minutes

Serving size: 2 servings
Prep time: 10 minutes
Cook Time: 15 minutes

Ingredients:
- ¼ cup of cannabis cooking oil
- 1 large potato
- 1 tablespoon salt or 1 tablespoon popcorn seasoning of your choice

Equipment:
- Large baking sheet
- Parchment paper
- Vegetable peeler
- Knife

Directions:
1. Set your oven temperature to 400° F and let it heat up while you prepare your potato chips.

2. Line the baking sheet with parchment paper to prevent your chips from sticking.

3. Peel the potato and slice it as thinly as possible into chips. Using a vegetable peeler to slice the chips is effective for achieving thin slices that will crisp well in the oven.

4. Spread out the potato chip slices evenly on your lined baking sheet and drizzle them with the cannabis oil infusion. Coat each chip evenly and well.

5. Place the baking sheet in the center of the preheated oven and bake for about 15 minutes or until golden brown and crispy.

6. Remove the baking sheet from the oven, sprinkle your salt or seasoning over them evenly to taste, and allow the potato chips to cool for about 5 minutes.

Buffalo Chex Mix

Time: 55 minutes
Serving size: 3 cups of buffalo Chex mix (serving size suggestion: ¾ cup of mix)
Prep time: 10 minutes
Cook Time: 45 minutes

Ingredients:
- ¾ cup Rice Chex cereal
- ¾ cup Corn Chex cereal
- ½ cup rye chips
- ¼ cup of peanuts
- ½ cup small cheddar cheese crackers such as Cheez-Its
- ½ cup pretzels
- ¾ tablespoon cannabis butter

- ¼ tablespoon regular butter
- 1 ounce buffalo sauce
- ¼ packet of dry powdered ranch dressing mix

Equipment:
- Large mixing bowl
- Medium saucepan
- Large baking sheet
- Parchment paper (optional)
- Non-stick cooking spray (optional)

Directions:
1. Switch your oven on to 250° F and allow it to preheat while you prepare the mix for baking.

2. Spray a large baking sheet with non-stick cooking spray or, alternatively, line it with a piece of parchment paper and set it aside.

3. In a large mixing bowl, toss the peanuts, crackers, pretzels, both types of Chex cereal, and rye chips and set aside.

4. Set a medium saucepan over medium heat and melt the cannabis butter and regular butter together. Once the butters are melted and combined, mix in the buffalo sauce.

5. Pour the butter and buffalo sauce mixture over the dry ingredients in the mixing bowl and toss well to thoroughly and evenly coat the ingredients.

6. Pour the Chex mix onto your prepared baking sheet, spreading it out evenly in a single layer, and sprinkle the dry ranch dressing over the mix.

7. Place the baking sheet in the center of the oven and bake for 45 minutes. Stir the mix every 15 minutes to prevent clumping and ensure an even bake.

8. Once baked, remove the baking sheet from the oven and place on a countertop to cool. Allow to cool completely and store the buffalo Chex mix in an airtight container for up to one week.

Baked Kale Chips

Time: 20 minutes plus cooling time
Serving size: 2 servings of kale chips
Prep time: 10 minutes
Cook Time: 10 minutes

Ingredients:
- 1/2 bunch of kale
- 1/2 tablespoon of cannabis butter
- Salt to taste or seasoning spices of your choice

Equipment:
- Baking sheet
- Parchment paper
- Heat-proof ramekin

Directions:
1. Preheat your oven by setting the temperature to 375° F and ensure that the oven rack is placed in the

center.

2. Line the baking sheet with a piece of parchment paper and set it aside.

3. Wash and thoroughly dry the kale leaves. Remove the stalk from each leaf and then tear each leaf into pieces. The leaf pieces should be around twice the size of a regular tortilla chip. Don't worry if this seems like it's a bit big, the kale chips will shrink in size as they bake so you want to make the raw chips bigger than you want the final baked chips to be.

4. Place the kale chips on the lined baking tray, spreading them out as evenly as possible and ensuring that they form only one layer with no overlapping.

5. Melt the cannabis butter in the ramekin using a microwave. This will only take a few seconds. Alternatively, you can place the ramekin in the preheating oven to melt the butter.

6. Drizzle the melted cannabutter over your spread-out kale leaves. If the coverage isn't sufficient, add some extra regular butter or some olive oil.

7. To ensure even coverage and a better finished kale chip, massage the drizzled butter into each piece of kale leaf. However, you can skip this step if it seems like too much work.

8. Sprinkle the kale with salt or seasoning spices of your choice.

9. Place the baking sheet into the oven and bake the kale for roughly 8 to 10 minutes or until the chips are browned but have not burned.

10. Once baked, remove the baking sheet from the oven and set aside on a countertop to cool off. The kale chips will become crispier as they cool.

11. Store any leftover kale chips in a single layer and cover loosely. Contrary to storage instructions for many other snack foods, don't store your leftovers in an airtight container, as this will cause them to lose their crisp.

Hush Puppies

Time: 45 minutes
Serving size: Dependent on the size of batter dollops
Prep time: 15 minutes
Cook Time: 30 minutes

Ingredients:
- 6 cups of your preferred regular cooking oil
- 1 cup of cannabis milk
- 1 ½ cups of self-rising cornmeal
- ½ teaspoon salt
- ½ cup self-rising flour, all-purpose
- ½ teaspoon baking soda
- 1 beaten egg

Equipment:
- Deep fryer
- Mixing bowls
- Teaspoon

Directions:

1. Switch the deep fryer on and add the cooking oil, allowing it to heat up to 350° F.

2. Combine the dry ingredients in a mixing bowl and mix well.

3. Using a second mixing bowl, combine the cannabis milk and egg, mixing until incorporated.

4. Add the wet ingredients to the bowl with the dry ingredients and mix thoroughly.

5. Use a teaspoon to scoop out batter and drop it into the hot oil in small dollops. Fry the dollops of batter, turning once, until each side is a rich golden brown color.

6. Be careful not to overcrowd the fryer or to burn the hush puppies. Frying smaller batches at a time offers you better control over the cooking process.

7. Fry all of the batter until finished.

8. Remove each batch of fried hush puppies and lay them between two layers of paper town to absorb any excess oil.

9. Serve warm and enjoy.

No-Bake Cannabis Cookie Bars

Ingredients:
- 1/2 cup melted cannabis butter
- 1 1/2 cups Graham cracker crumbs
- One pound confectioners' sugar (3 to 3 1/2 cups)
- 1 1/2 cups peanut butter
- 1/2 cup butter, melted
- 1 (12 ounces) bag milk chocolate chips

Directions:
1. Combine Graham cracker crumbs, sugar and peanut butter; mix well.
2. Blend in the melted cannabis butter until well combined .

3. Press mixture evenly into a 9 x 13-inch pan.

4. Melt chocolate chips in microwave or in a double boiler.

5. Spread over peanut butter mixture.

6. Chill until just set and cut into bars. (These are very hard to cut if the chocolate gets "rock hard"

Chocolate Bananas

Ingredients:
- ½ cup cannabutter
- 3 ripe but firm bananas
- 1 pound dark chocolate, chopped, or semisweet chocolate chips
- 1/2 cup granola, chopped pecans and walnuts, or sprinkles (optional)

Directions :
1. Line a baking sheet with nonstick foil or parchment paper.
2. Cut the bananas in half and insert a popsicle stick into each half, as shown.

3. Place them on the baking sheet and freeze for 15 minutes.

4. Melt the cannabutter over a low heat and then set it aside.

5. Melt chocolate in the same double boiler until smooth. Add the cannabutter to the chocolate as it's melting. Gently mix the cannabutter into the chocolate.

6. Roll each banana half in the chocolate, then quickly sprinkle with your topping (if using).

7. Freeze until the chocolate sets, 30 minutes.

8. Serve and then enjoy! Or freeze in an airtight container for up to a week.

Creamy Stuffed Cannabis-Infused Pancakes

Ingredients:
- 1 cup cannabis milk
- 1 egg
- 2 tablespoons vegetable oil
- 1 teaspoon salt
- 2 tablespoons sugar
- 1 cup flour
- 2 teaspoons baking powder (for the filling)
- 1 cup cream cheese
- Chopped strawberries
- Blueberries
- 2 tablespoons vanilla sugar
- 1/2 cup whipping cream

Directions :
1. In a large bowl, sift together the flour, baking powder, salt, and sugar. Make a well in the center and pour in the milk, egg and vegetable oil; mix until smooth.
2. Heat a lightly oiled griddle or frying pan over medium-high to low heat. Pour or scoop the batter onto the griddle. Brown on both sides and serve hot.

For Filling:
1. In a medium mixing bowl, beat the softened cream cheese until smooth.
2. Add whipping cream and vanilla. Beat mixture until combined. Stir in both berries and sugar.

3. To serve, spoon 2/3 tablespoons of filling onto each thin pancake.

4. Serve with chocolate sauce.

Chocolate Weed Brownies

Ingredients:
- 1/4 cup cannabis butter
- 1/4 cup normal butter
- 2 eggs
- 1 teaspoon vanilla extract
- 1/3 cup unsweetened cocoa powder
- 1/2 cup all-purpose flour
- 1/4 teaspoon salt
- 1/4 teaspoon baking powder

For the Frosting:
- 3 tablespoons butter, softened
- 1 teaspoon cannabis butter, softened
- 1 tablespoon honey
- 1 teaspoon vanilla extrac t
- 1 cup confectioners' sugar

Directions:
1. Preheat oven to 330 degrees F.
2. Grease and flour an 8-inch square pan.

3. In a large saucepan, on very low heat, melt 1/4 cup butter and 1/4 cup cannabis butter. Remove from heat, and stir in sugar, eggs and 1 teaspoon vanilla. Beat in 1/3 cup cocoa, 1/2 cup flour, salt and baking powder. Spread batter into prepared pan.

4. Bake in preheated oven for 25 to 30 minutes. Do not overcook.

For the Frosting:
1. Combine 3 tablespoons softened butter and 1 teaspoon cannabis butter; add 3 tablespoons cocoa, honey, 1 teaspoon vanilla extract, and 1 cup confectioners' sugar. Stir until smooth.
2. Frost brownies while they are still warm.

How to Make Weed Candy

Time Required: 25 minutes
Yield: 3 to 4 dozen pieces
Ingredients:

- 2 cups sugar

- 1¼ cup cannabis corn syrup

- 1 cup water

- Food coloring/flavoring of your choice

Directions:
1. Heat sugar, cannabis corn syrup and water in saucepan over medium heat.
2. Stir until all sugars are dissolved. Bring to a 300 degree boil.

3. Add food coloring and flavoring slowly. Stir well.

4. Turn off heat. Carefully and quickly pour liquid into candy molds before it hardens.

5. Remove candy from mold once it is finished cooling. Toss candy in sugar, if desired.

Cannabis Caramel Candy

Time Required: 25 minutes
Yield: 3 to 4 dozen pieces
Ingredients:
- 1 cup cannabutter

- 2 ¼ cups brown sugar

- Dash salt

- 1 cup light corn syrup

- 14 ounces sweetened condensed milk (canned)

- 1 teaspoon vanilla extract

Directions:
1. Melt cannabutter slowly in saucepan .
2. Stir in brown sugar and salt until combined.

3. Stir in light corn syrup.

4. Add milk slowly while constantly stirring.

5. Cook mixture over medium heat until candy begins to get firmer (usually 12 to 15 minutes).

6. Remove saucepan from heat and stir in the vanilla extract.

7. Pour mixture into 9x13 pan. Allow candy to cool down.

8. Cut, serve and store.

Caramel Cashew Squares

Ingredients:
> For Crust:
- 1/3 cup firmly packed brown sugar

- 4 tablespoons butter (2 cannabutter, 2 regular)

- 1 cup all-purpose flour

- 1/4 teaspoon sal t

  <u>For Topping:</u>
- 1/2 cup butterscotch-flavored baking chips

- 1/4 cup light corn syrup

- 2 tablespoons cannabutter

- 1 cup chopped salted cashews

Directions:

1. Heat oven to 350°F.

2. Place brown sugar in medium bowl.

3. Add 4 tablespoons of butter, and mix with brown sugar in a blender until it resembles coarse crumbs.

4. Add flour and salt. Mix well.

5. Press mixture onto bottom of the ungreased 8-inch square baking pan.

6. Bake for 11-13 minutes and let set.

7. Melt butterscotch chips, corn syrup and 2 tablespoons cannabutter in 2-quart saucepan over low heat, stirring occasionally.

8. Remove from heat. Stir in cashews.

9. Pour cashew mixture over the crust.

10. Continue baking for 8-10 minutes or until it starts to bubble.

 Set and cool completely.

11. Cover; store refrigerated. Cut into bars.

Homemade Cannabis Oreo Cookies

Ingredients:

- 1 cup 50/50 butter/cannabis butter mixed

- 1 cup sugar

- 2 teaspoons salt

- 2 large eggs

- 2 cups all-purpose flour

- 1 ¼ cups dark cocoa powder

- ½ teaspoon baking soda

<u>For Cream Filling:</u>

- ½ cup cannabis butter

- 2 cups powdered sugar
- 1 teaspoon vanilla

Directions :

1. Preheat oven to 325 degrees F .

2. In a large bowl, cream together 1/2 cup cannabis butter with ½ cup normal butter. Mix with the white sugar and salt until light and fluffy.

3. Beat in eggs until fully incorporated.

4. Sieve together the flour, cocoa powder, and baking soda into the mix. Blend well.

5. Add the dry ingredients to the wet ingredients, and mix together until combined.

6. Turn the dough out onto your surface and push together into a flat square. Wrap the dough in plastic wrap and refrigerate for 1 hour.

<u>For Cream Filling:</u>

1. To make the filling, combine ½ cup cannabis butter, powdered sugar, and vanilla in a medium mixing bowl. Beat together until light and fluffy.

2. Remove the dough from the fridge, and for ease of rolling out, divide the dough into 4 pieces.

3. To roll out the dough, place a quarter of the dough between two sheets of parchment paper. Roll the dough between the two sheets of parchment to ¼-inch thickness .

4. Using a small round cookie cutter or champagne glass, cut the dough into individual rounds and place on a large parchment-lined baking sheet, leaving at least ½-inch between each cookie.

5. Pack together and re-roll out any scraps to cut additional cookies. Repeat this process with each remaining ¼ of the dough.

6. Bake in preheated oven for 15 minutes.

7. Remove and transfer cookies to a cooling rack to cool completely.

8. Assemble the cookies by spreading a generous scoop of the icing onto one of the cookies and sandwiching it with another. Give it a light squeeze and scrape any excess off to clear and even out the sides.

9. Serve with a glass of milk.

Cannabis Chocolate Ice Cream with Super Potent Blondies

Ingredients:
- 4 tablespoons cannabis butter
- 1 can condensed milk
- 1 teaspoon vanilla extract
- 1/2 cup cocoa powder
- 2 cups heavy cream

- 1/2 cup cannabis butter

- 1 cup light brown suga r

- 1 egg

- 1 teaspoon vanilla extract

- 1 cup flour

- 1/2 teaspoon baking powder

- 1/8 teaspoon baking soda

- Pinch of salt

- 1 cup white chocolate

Directions:
1. Preheat oven to 220 degrees F.
2. In a medium bowl, mix your condensed milk, 4 tablespoons cannabis butter, vanilla and cocoa powder; set aside.

3. In another bowl, whip your whipping cream until stiff.

4. Fold your chocolate mixture into your whipping cream mixture using a spatula.

5. Freeze for at least 6 hours

6. In a medium bowl, mix together your cannabis butter with brown sugar using an electric hand mixer.

7. Add your egg and vanilla and mix again.

8. Now add your flour, baking powder, baking soda and salt; mix again.

9. Fold in your white chocolate using a spatula.

 Place your mixture on a floured baking tray and bake for 40 minutes.

10. Serve little chunks on your chocolate ice cream.

Cannabis Chocolate Caramel Peanut Butter Cups

Ingredients:
- 4 tablespoons cannabis butter

- 2 1/2 cups chocolate

- 1/2 cup salted caramel sauce

- 1 cup peanut butte r

- 1/2 cup powdered sugar

- 1/4 cup cornflakes

- Pinch of salt

Directions:

1. Take a medium bowl and melt chocolate au bain marie with your cannabis butter.

2. Mix using a spatula so your cannabis butter is evenly mixed into the chocolate.

3. Put your chocolate cannabis mix in a piping bag and let cool slightly.

4. Line up a tray with 12 paper cupcake cups.

5. Use half of your chocolate cannabis mix to fill out the cups evenly. A thin layer just so the bottom is covered will do.

6. Freeze for 5 minutes until chocolate is solid.

7. Add a good tablespoon of caramel sauce to each chocolate cup.

8. Freeze again for 5 minutes

9. In a medium small bowl, mix 1 cup peanut butter with the cornflakes, powdered sugar and cannabis butter using a hand mixer.

10. Add a full tablespoon of peanut butter to your chocolate cups.

11. Now use the other half of your cannabis chocolate to cover the peanut butter.

12. Freeze for about 15 - 20 minutes.

13. Serve.

Potent Cannabis Brownies

Ingredients:
- 1 cup cannabis butter
- 2/3 cup chocolate
- 1 teaspoon vanilla extract
- Orange zest (optional)
- 5 egg whites
- 4 egg yolk s
- 3/4 cup sugar
- 1/3 cup flour
- 1 tablespoon cocoa powder
- 1/2 cup crushed pecan nuts

Directions:
1. Preheat oven to 220 degrees F.
2. Use a double boiler by placing a bowl on top of a pot with water over medium high heat.

3. Add your chocolate, cannabis butter, vanilla extract and orange zest to the empty bowl and mix to incorporate.

4. Take the bowl off the heat and set aside. (You will not need any heat anymore from this point on.)

5. Place your egg whites in a separate bowl.

6. Beat egg whites until you form stiff white peaks, using an electric mixer or a whisk; set aside.

7. Add your egg yolks to another separate bowl and add sugar. Mix to incorporate.

8. Add your chocolate cannabis mixture to the egg-yolk mixture and slowly incorporate both using a spatula.

9. Once incorporated, sift in your flour, cocoa powder and add your pecan nuts.

10. Now add your fluffy white egg whites to the mixture, and incorporate everything together using a spatula .

11. Line a baking pan with parchment paper and add your finished mixture to it.

12. Now bake for 60 minutes, and your brownies will be ready.

Cannabis-Infused Ice Cream

Ingredients:
- 4 tablespoons cannabis butter
- 2 cups whipping cream
- 1 can (14oz) condensed milk
- 1/2 teaspoon vanilla extract
- 1/4 cup chopped mint

Directions:
1. Whip the cream until stiff; add all remaining ingredients in separate bowl and mix.
2. Now fold the mixture into the whipping cream. Store in a container and freeze for 6 hours.

3. Serve the cannabis Ice cream.

Weed Banana Bread

Prep Time: 5 minutes
Cook Time: 50-60 minutes
Serves:10-12
Recommended Dosage: 3 tablespoons cannabutter
Ingredients:
- 2 cups flour
- 1/2 cup sugar
- 1 teaspoon baking soda
- 1/2 teaspoon salt

- 1 1/2 cups mashed ripe bananas

- 1/4 cup honey or agave nectar (lower glycemic index)

- 1/4 cup sour cream

- 2 large eggs, lightly beaten

- 6 tablespoons melted butter

- 1 teaspoon vanilla

- 1 1/4 cups toasted and chopped pecans

Directions:
1. Preheat oven to 350 degrees F. Grease and flour a 9X5 inch loaf pan and set aside.
2. In a medium bowl, combine the flour, sugar, baking soda and salt; then, mix well and set aside. In a large bowl, mix the mashed bananas, honey, sour cream, eggs, melted butter and vanilla.

3. Lightly fold the dry ingredients into the wet ingredients, mixing only until incorporated. Stir in the chopped pecans. Batter will be lumpy.

4. Pour batter into prepared pan and bake for 50-60 minutes, or until a tester comes out clean.

5. Cool in pan for 5 minutes, then transfer to a wire rack to cool completely.

OMFG MINT CANNABIS BROWNIES

Ingredients:
- 1 cup cannabutter

- 6 ounces unsweetened chocolate

- 2 cups sugar

- 1 teaspoon baking powder

- 1½ teaspoons vanilla

- ½ teaspoon salt

- 1½ cups flou r

- 1 cup walnuts or pecans, finely ground

- 1 1/2 ounces bag Hershey's mint chocolate chips

- 4 eggs

Directions:
1. Preheat oven to
2. In a medium saucepan, melt cannabutter and unsweetened chocolate over low heat, stirring constantly. Remove from heat and let cool.

3. Grease 9×13 inch pan and set aside. Stir sugar into cooled chocolate mixture in saucepan. Beat eggs, and add slowly to chocolate mixture. Stir in vanilla.

4. In a bowl, stir together the flour, baking soda and salt.

5. Add flour mixture to chocolate mixture until combined. Stir in nuts and mint chocolate chips. Spread the batter in the prepared pan.

6. Bake for 30 minutes. Cool on wire rack before storing.

Poppy-Pot Cake

Ingredients:

For Cake :

- 1 3/4 cups cannaflour

- 1/2 teaspoon baking powder

- 1/2 teaspoon baking soda

- 1/8 teaspoon salt

- 1/2 cup unsalted cannabutter, softened

- 1 1/4 cups sugar

- 3 eggs

- 1 cup creme fraiche

- 3 tablespoons poppy seeds

- 1/2 teaspoon almond extract

For Frosting:

- 4 ounces cream cheese, softened

- 2/3 cup powdered suga r

- 1 cup creme fraiche

- 1 teaspoon finely grated lemon peel

- 1/8 teaspoon almond extract

Directions:

1. Preheat oven to 350 degrees F. Spray bottom of a 9-inch square pan with nonstick cooking spray.

2. In a medium bowl, stir together cannaflour, baking powder, baking soda and salt.

3. In a large bowl, beat butter at a medium speed for 30 seconds, until creamy. Add sugar, beat for 5 minutes or until light, creamy and fluffy. Add eggs one at a time, beating until blended.

4. At low speed, beat in flour mixture in 3 parts alternately, with 1 cup creme fraiche, beginning and ending with flour mixture. Beat in poppy seeds and 1/2 teaspoon almond extract.

5. Spoon and spread batter into pan (It will be very thick). Bake 35-40 minutes or until dark golden brown and toothpick inserted in center comes out clean. Cool completely on wire rack.

6. Right before serving, in another large bowl, beat cream cheese and powdered sugar at low speed until smooth. Slowly beat in 1 cup creme fraiche until blended. Increase speed to medium; beat frosting until firm, but do not let stiff peaks form. Beat in lemon peel and 1/8 teaspoon almond extract.

7. Spread frosting over cake. Store in refrigerator.

Purple Kush Cake

Ingredients:

- ¾ cup THC oil1

- 25 ounce Betty Crocker Super Moist Dark Chocolate Mix

- 3 eggs

- 2 cups cold milk

- One 16-ounce tub Betty Crocker Rich & Creamy Vanilla Frosting

Directions:

1. Preheat oven to 400 degrees F.
2. Mix together the cake referencing the package directions. Use the infused oil instead of cooking oil and mix it with the eggs and water.

3. Pour the cake mixture into 2 evenly sized pans, and bake for 30 minutes or until a knife comes out of the cake clean.

4. Mix the frosting until smooth and spread a layer over the top of one cake. Put the other cake on top to create a cake sandwich. Now smother the entire cake in frosting and enjoy!

Fire Crackers

Ingredients:

- **Weed** : A bowl (0.3 to 2 grams) per firecracker. The amount you will want to use depends on your tolerance. Use the same amount you would normally smoke. We estimate this at about half a gram all the way up to 2 grams for those who pack tight and smoke to great heights for each firecracker you are going to make. We are going to eat our firecrackers for medical purposes so we are choosing a medical strain, Harlequin. It has a floral taste like a bouquet of flowers, perfect for our peanut butter and Nutella cookie sandwiches.

- **Saltine crackers** : Choose your favorite cracker. Since you will be adding peanut butter, you may want to choose a cracker with less sugar so that it doesn't taste so much like a cookie. You also want a cracker, a Graham or Ritz cracker, that can withstand a little baking without coming apart.

- **Peanut Butter** : Choose your favorite peanut butter. You may want to go organic with less sugar. It's important that the peanut butter has mostly natural peanut oil rather than soybean oil, although soybean oil will still work.

- **Nutella** : You can use Nutella only or peanut butter only or mix them. Nutella is a hazelnut and chocolate spread. It is mostly hazel nut but also has cocoa in it. Some people love the taste.

Directions:

1. Preheat oven to 250 degrees F.

2. Decarb your weed. The first thing you want to do is decarb your weed. Decarboxylating your weed is going to convert inactive THCA to potent THC. Now, take your gram or more of weed, and place it in the oven for ten minutes. Now your Harlequin weed is activated, full of THC and CBD. It will look a bit brown and toasted. It should smell really dank, pungent, and delicious.

3. Spread peanut butter and Nutella on your cracker. You may want to put peanut butter on one cracker and Nutella on another .

4. Add 0.3 to 2 grams of decarbed weed into the peanut butter on the cracker. Mix it in. The oil in the peanut butter is going to extract the cannabinoids, so make sure you mix it in good into the peanut butter side because it has the most reliable oils. Now, put one cracker on top of the other.

5. Wrap your sandwiched crackers in tin foil. The foil will protect your cannabinoids from evaporating away.

6. Raise the temperature to 300 degrees F. Bake your weed firecrackers in a toaster oven for 15 minutes.

7. Remove. Let it cool on your plate.

8. Your firecracker is ready to be consumed. It's that simple…you've made your easiest weed edible to make. But don't let the ease of baking fool you, this edible is as powerful as the weed you put in it, so be mindful of how much weed you have used and how much THC it has. Respect the weed and you will have a great time.

Blueberry Cannabis Pie

Ingredients:

- 2 sheets of refrigerated pie crusts
- 5 cups fresh blueberries
- 1 cup sugar
- ½ cup cannaflour
- ½ teaspoon ground cinnamon
- 2 tablespoons butter, melted
- 1 large egg, beate n
- 1 teaspoon sugar

Directions:

1. Preheat oven to 375 degrees F.

2. Press one pie crust sheet firmly into the bottom of a 9 inch pie dish and up the sides of the pan.

3. Trim the edge of the dough with kitchen scissors; leave 1 inch of dough to hang over edge of pan. Set aside.

4. Stir together the blueberries, cannaflour, sugar, butter, egg and cinnamon.

5. Transfer the filling mix to the dough-lined pan.

6. Place the second pie sheet over the filled pie. Trim edges appropriately, leaving 1 inch of dough hanging.

7. Fold the edge of the top layer of dough under the edge of the bottom layer of dough. Pinch dough sheets together to seal.

8. Cut an 'x' across the top center of the dough to allow steam to escape.

9. Put the uncooked pie in the refrigerator to firm the dough (about 20 minutes).

10. Remove pie from refrigerator and bake the pie in the preheated oven for 1 hour, or until the crust is golden brown and the filling is bubbling.

11. Transfer pie to a wire rack and let cool for at least 1 hour before serving.

Cinnamon Pecan Sandies

Ingredients:
- 1 cup ground pecans
- 1 cup cannabutter
- 2 cups all-purpose flour
- ½ teaspoon baking powder
- 1 tablespoon vanilla extract
- 1 cup natural brown sugar
- 2 teaspoons cinnamon
- ½ cup sifted powdered sugar

Directions:
1. Preheat oven to 352 degrees F .
2. Cream the cannabutter and sugar together in a mixing bowl until smooth. While creaming, add in the vanilla. Sift together the flour and baking powder and gradually add it to your mixing bowl. Add the chopped pecans. Cover the dough and chill for 3-4 hours.

3. Remove the dough from the refrigerator and roll it into golf-sized balls before gently flattening them in your hand and placing them on an ungreased cookie sheet.

4. Bake for about 20 minutes or until slightly firm and golden. Remove from the oven and gently placing them on a cooling rack.

5. Combine the sifted powdered sugar and cinnamon and dust them with the mixture. Allow them to completely cool to avoid crumbling. Enjoy!

Cheech and Chong's Chocolate Cake.

Ingredients:

- 1 cup dark chocolate

- 1 cup cannabutter

- 1 1/2 cups caster sugar, plus an extra pinch

- 6 eggs, separated into yolks and whites

- 1/2 cup ground almonds

- 3/4 cup soft white breadcrumbs

- 1/8 cup plain flour

- 4 teaspoons vanilla essence

- <u>For the Icing:</u>
- 3/8 cup cocoa powde r

- 1 cup icing sugar

- 2/3 cup butter

- 3/4 cup caster sugaz

- 6 tablespoons water

Directions:

<u>For the Space Cake:</u>
1. Preheat the oven to 325 degrees F. Grease and line a 10 inch round cake tin.
2. Melt the chocolate in a double boiler or in a bowl placed over a pan of boiling water.

3. Cream the cannabis butter with 1 1/2 cups sugar until pale and softened.

4. Gradually beat in the egg yolks and stir in the almonds. Fold in the cool melted chocolate, breadcrumbs, flour and vanilla essence.

5. In a separate bowl, whip the egg whites with a pinch of sugar until stiff but not dry. Fold into the cake mixture and pour into the prepared cake tin.

6. Bake for 1 hour until firm to the touch.

<u>For the Icing:</u>

1. Sieve the cocoa and icing sugar into a bowl.
2. Warm the butter, sugar and water in a microwave or double boiler and simmer until the sugar has dissolved .

3. Add the liquid to the dry mixture and combine until thickened.

4. Spread the icing over the cooled hash cake.

Twice-Cooked Popcorn Bars

Ingredients:

- 8 tablespoons cannabutter

- 6 cups marshmallows or mini marshmallows, don't count, it's a bag!

- 5 tablespoons peanut butter

- 7-8 cups popped caramel corn or popcorn

- 1 cup peanuts, chopped

- 1 cup mini chocolate chips

- <u>For Topping:</u>
- ½ cup mini marshmallows

- ½ cup mini chocolate chips

Directions :

1. Heat oven to 350 degrees F.

2. Cover the bottom of a 9-inch square pan with parchment paper.

3. In a large saucepan melt the butter. Add the marshmallows and stir until fully melted. Stir in the peanut butter.

4. Add the popcorn and mix until evenly coated. Spread half the mixture into prepared pan. With damp clean hands, press the popcorn down and try to make even thickness. Sprinkle with the peanuts and the chocolate chips.

5. Press the remaining popcorn mixture on top of the peanuts and chocolate.

6. Sprinkle with the remaining marshmallows and chocolate chips, and place in the oven for 5-7 minutes.

7. Allow to cool and then chill in refrigerator before cutting.

Peppermint Buddha Bark

Ingredients:
- 12 ounces white chocolate

- 6 ounces semisweet chocolate

- 4 tablespoons cannabis-infused coconut oil

- ½ teaspoon peppermint extract

- 3 candy canes (crushed)

Directions :

1. Line a 9×9 inch baking pan with some parchment paper or aluminum foil, making sure to wrap the foil over the sides of the pan, and smooth out any wrinkles as you go. This step will ensure a quick clean up and will also allow for the peppermint bark to easily pop off the pan when it comes time to break it into individual pieces.

2. Melt together the semisweet chocolate chips and the white chocolate chips. To do this, create a double boiler using a heat-safe bowl and a saucepan filled with water. Choose a bowl that fits snugly over the top of the saucepan (Do not use a bowl that sits precariously on top of the pot). You also want to ensure that the bottom of the bowl does not touch the water or you risk burning the chocolate.

3. As an aside, this recipe uses 3 layers of chocolate for the bark (white, semisweet, white). Feel free to switch up the quantities of the chocolate and reverse the layering (semisweet, white, semisweet) if you so please!

4. Bring the water in the saucepan to a simmer, and place the heat-safe bowl containing your white chocolate chips over the sauce pan.

5. Melt the white chocolate chips until they're smooth .

6. Add in 4 tablespoons of cannabis-infused coconut oil and the ½ teaspoon of peppermint extract.

7. Stir until both oils have fully dissolved into the white chocolate. Aside from medicating the dish, the coconut oil will also create a nice shine in the bark and allow it to have a good "snap" when breaking up the pieces.

8. Once the melted white chocolate is smooth again, pour half of it into the prepped pan. Tilt the pan after you pour in half of the melted white chocolate to ensure an even coating/first layer.

9. Place the pan in the refrigerator and allow the first layer of chocolate to harden completely, roughly 30 minutes or so.

10. While your first layer of bark is setting, repeat the above steps in order to prepare a second double boiler for your semi-sweet chocolate chips.

11. Once your semisweet chocolate chips are completely melted, remove the bowl from the double boiler.

12. Take the pan containing the first layer of white chocolate from the refrigerator and proceed to pour the entire bowl of melted semisweet chocolate chips over the first layer. It is extremely important that the initial layer of white chocolate is completely hardened, as introducing the second layer will cause them to mix if this is not the case .

13. Spread the second layer of semisweet chocolate chips evenly throughout the pan using a spatula or baker's knife.

14. Place the pan back into the refrigerator as you wait for the second layer of chocolate to set, again roughly 30 minutes or so.

15. When the second layer of chocolate has set, add the third and final layer of white chocolate on top of the semisweet layer. Spread this third layer evenly with a spatula.

16. Place the candy canes into a Ziploc bag and proceed to crush them into tiny pieces using the back of a ladle or a rolling pin.

17. Sprinkle the crushed candy canes on top of the third and final layer of white chocolate covering the entire surface, and then place the pan back into the refrigerator until the bark is completely set (30 minutes to 1 hour).

18. When ready to eat, remove the bark from the refrigerator and pull up on the sides of the aluminum foil – the bark should lift right out of the pan!

19. Break the bark into individual pieces, and either package them up to give as a gift, or serve them to your guests immediately!

Butterscotch Cannabis Blondies

Ingredients:

- 1 cup marijuana butter

- 4 cups brown sugar

- 4 eggs

- 1 teaspoon vanilla

- 2 cups unbleached white flour

- 1 teaspoon baking powder

- 2 teaspoons sea sal t

- 2 cups chopped mixed nuts (unsalted)

Directions:

1. Preheat oven to

2. This recipe is full of sugar - brown sugar, that is. It takes well to spelt flour or other alternatives to wheat flour. Be sure to experiment with a bit of your dough and taste to make sure the flour alternative does not adversely affect the flavor of your recipe.

3. Melt the marijuana butter in a large saucepan.

4. Add the brown sugar, and stir until gloppy. Take off the heat immediately.

5. Place the saucepan on a hot pad and allow the mixture to cool slightly. Add the eggs slowly, making sure that the heat of the mixture does not coagulate the egg.

6. Add the vanilla and mix thoroughly.

7. Add the flour, baking powder and salt and mix well. Stir in the chopped mixed nuts.

8. Pour into a greased 13x24 inch baking pan.

9. Bake 45 minutes or until done. Do not overbake!

Almond Lemon Bars

Ingredients:

- 1/4 cup granulated sugar

- 3/4 cup cannabis-infused butter (softened)

- 1 teaspoon lemon zest

- 2 cups all-purpose flour

- 1/4 teaspoon table sal t

  For Lemon Bar Batter:

- 6 large eggs

- 2 cups sugar

- 1/4 cup chopped, crystallized ginger

- 1/2 cup all-purpose flour

- 1 teaspoon baking powder

- 2 tablespoons lemon zest

- 2/3 cup fresh lemon juice

For Almond Mixture:
- 3/4 cup flour

- 1/2 cup sugar

- 1/4 teaspoon salt

- 1/4 cup cannabis-infused butter (melted)

- 1/2 cup sliced almonds

- Optional garnishes: a dusting of powdered sugar, whipped cream, etc.

Directions:

For Lemon Bar Crust:
1. Preheat your oven to 350 degrees F.
2. Using a standing or hand-held electric mixer, beat 1/4 cup of sugar, 3/4 cup of softened cannabis-infused butter and 1 teaspoon of lemon zest at medium speed for 2 minutes or until the mixture is creamy .

3. In a separate large bowl, combine 2 cups of flour and 1/4 teaspoon of salt. Gradually add the dry goods (flour and salt) to the creamed butter, sugar and eggs. Mix well until everything is thoroughly combined.

4. After the dough crust is mixed, prep a 9x13 inch baking dish with some nonstick cooking spray. Place the empty, greased dish into the refrigerator to chill for at least 15 minutes prior to baking.

5. Remove the dish from the refrigerator, and press the dough into the pan until you create a uniform layer. (Don't miss the corners!)

6. Bake the crust for 15 to 20 minutes in your preheated oven or until lightly browned.

7. Remove the crust from the oven and reduce the oven temperature to 325 degrees F.

8. Let the crust sit to the side for now.

For Lemon Bar Batter:
1. Whisk together the 6 eggs and 2 cups of sugar.
2. In a food processor or blender, pour in the 1/2 cup of flour along with the 1/4 cup of crystallized ginger. Pulse the two ingredients together until fully combined. Proceed to pour the flour and ginger blend into a medium size bowl.

3. Stir 1 teaspoon of baking powder into the flour and ginger blend .

4. Slowly add batches of the flour and ginger blend to the bowl containing the eggs and sugar.

5. Whisk in the lemon juice and 2 tablespoons of lemon zest until fully combined and smooth.

6. Pour the lemon bar batter over the cooled crust, shimmying and jiggling the dish to allow any air bubbles to escape.

7. Bake the lemon bars in your preheated oven for 15 to 20 minutes or until the lemon filling has just barely set.

8. Remove the lemon bars from the oven and place them to the side for now.

For Sliced Almond Mixture:
1. Stir the remaining 3/4 cup flour, 1/2 cup of sugar and 1/4 teaspoon of salt together in a small bowl.
2. Pour in the 1/4 cup of melted cannabis-infused butter, and stir the ingredients until they're well blended.

3. Add the 1/2 cup of sliced almonds, and stir once more.

4. Sprinkle the almond and sugar mixture over the hot lemon bars, and then place the lemon bars back into the oven for an additional 20 to 25 minutes or until they're lightly golden in color .

5. Remove the lemon bars from the oven and allow them to cool in the baking dish on top of a wire cooling rack for at least 1 hour.

6. Cut your lemon bars into individual squares, and serve immediately with a dash of powdered sugar, if you so please.

7. Enjoy.

Dank Cheesecake

Ingredients:
- 1/3 cup cannabutter, softened
- 1 (9 oz) premade Graham cracker crust
- 2 (8 oz) packages cream cheese, softened
- ¾ cup white sugar
- 1/3 cup milk
- 2 eggs
- ½ cup sour cream
- 1 ½ teaspoons vanilla extrac t
- 2 tablespoons all-purpose flour

Directions:
1. Heat oven to 350 degrees F. Remove plastic from premade crust.
2. With an electric mixer, mix cannabutter, cream cheese and sugar until combined. Add milk, eggs, sour cream, vanilla and flour. Mix until combined. Pour mixture into crust.

3. Bake 1 hour. Turn off heat. Leave cheesecake in closed oven for 5 hours.

4. Store in refrigerator.

Flourless Canna Chocolate Cake

Time Required: 9 hours
Prep Time: 20 minutes
Cook Time: 45 minutes
Ingredients:

- ½ cup cannabutter, melted

- ½ cup real butter, melted

- ½ cup water

- ¼ tsp salt

- ¾ cup white sugar

- 18 (1 oz) pieces bittersweet Baker's chocolate

- 6 egg s

Directions:

1. Heat oven to 300 degrees F. Spray a 10" pie dish with nonstick spray.

2. In a saucepan and on medium heat, stir water, sugar and salt until everything has dissolved. Remove from heat.

3. Microwave chocolate until melted. Be careful not to burn it.

4. With an electric mixer, mix melted chocolate, cannabutter, real butter and sugar mixture until combined. Mix in the eggs, two at a time until combined.

5. Pour mixture into pie dish. Set pie dish in a larger pan, and fill the larger pan with water until the water is ½ way to the top of the pie dish.

6. Bake 45 minutes.

7. Refrigerate 8 hours.

Coughing Coffee Cake

Time Required: 1 ¼ hours
Prep Time: 10 minutes
Cook Time: 55 minutes
Skip the morning coffee and try this for breakfast!
Ingredients:

- ½ cup cannabutter, melted

- ½ cup real butter, melted

- 1 (25 oz) box yellow cake mi x

- 1 (3.4 oz) box instant vanilla pudding mix

- 1 (3.4 oz) box instant butterscotch pudding mix

- 4 eggs

- 1 cup water

- 1 cup brown sugar

- 1 tablespoon ground cinnamon

Directions:
1. Heat oven to 350 degrees F. Spray a 9×13 baking dish with nonstick spray.
2. With an electric mixer, mix everything together (except brown sugar and cinnamon) until combined.

3. In a separate bowl, mix brown sugar and cinnamon until combined.

4. Pour ½ of cake mixture into baking dish. Evenly sprinkle ½ of brown sugar mixture on top. Pour in rest of cake mix. Evenly sprinkle the remaining brown sugar mix on top .

5. Bake 20 minutes. Then set heat to 325 degrees and bake 35 minutes. Let cool.

Chronic Carrot Cake

Ingredients:
For Cake:
- 2 cups all-purpose flour

- 1 teaspoon baking soda

- 2 teaspoons ground cinnamon

- 1/4 teaspoon salt

- 3 eggs

- 3/4 cup buttermilk

- 1 cup cannaoil

- 1 1/2 cups sugar

- 2 teaspoons vanilla extract

- 2 1/2 cups shredded carrot s

- 1 cup flaked coconut

- 1 cup chopped walnuts

- 1 cup raisins

For Frosting:
- 1/2 cup butter, softened (or cannabutter)

- 1 cup cream cheese (or canna cream cheese)

- 4 cups powdered sugar

- 1 teaspoon vanilla extract

Directions:

1. Preheat oven to 350 degrees F.

2. Sift together flour, baking soda, salt and cinnamon in a medium-sized bowl. Set aside.

3. Combine eggs, buttermilk, cannaoil, sugar and vanilla in a separate bowl, mix well.

4. Add flour mixture to the cannaoil mixture, stir well.

5. Combine shredded carrots, coconut, walnuts and raisins in a separate bowl.

6. Add carrot mixture to batter and mix thoroughly.

7. Pour batter into a greased cake pan and bake for 1 hour or until toothpick comes out clean.

8. Remove cake from oven and let cool.

9. Mix cream cheese, butter, milk and vanilla together while cake is cooling .

10. Frost cake with icing. Store in refrigerator.

11. In a medium bowl, combine butter, cream cheese, powdered sugar and vanilla extract to make the frosting. Beat until the mixture is smooth and creamy.

12. Frost the cooled cake. Cut and serve.

Pumpkin Roll-It-Up Cake

Time Required: 1 hour 40 minutes

Serves: 8

Ingredients:

    <u>Cake:</u>

- 1/4 cup confectioner's sugar for dusting towel

- 3/4 cup all-purpose flour

- 1/2 teaspoon baking powder

- 1/2 teaspoon baking soda

- 2 teaspoons pumpkin pie spice

- 1/4 teaspoon salt

- 3 large egg s

- 1 cup granulated sugar

- 2/3 cup canned pumpkin

    <u>For Filling:</u>

- 1 package cream cheese, softened, 8 ounces

- 3 tablespoons cannabis-infused butter, softened

- 5 tablespoons butter, softened

- 1 teaspoon vanilla extract

- 1 1/4 cups powdered sugar

Directions:

For Cake:

1. Preheat oven to 375° F. Grease a 12x17 inch jellyroll pan or cookie sheet with sides. Line pan with wax or parchment paper, and grease and flour the paper.
2. In a small bowl, combine the flour, baking powder, baking soda, pumpkin pie spice and salt.

3. In a large mixing bowl, beat eggs and sugar together with an electric mixer until thick and pale yellow, about 2 minutes. Stir in canned pumpkin until well combined. Stir in flour mixture just until combined.

4. Pour mixture into prepared pan.

5. Use a rubber spatula to smooth the batter out to the edges in an even layer, and bake 12 - 15 minutes or until cake springs back when touched.

6. While cake is baking, prepare clean kitchen towel by laying on the counter and dusting evenly with the powdered sugar.

7. When cake is done, immediately invert onto kitchen towel.

8. Peel off the parchment paper.

9. Starting at the shorter end of the towel, gently and loosely roll the cake inside of the towel. (The towel will be wrapped up inside the cake roll.) Move to a rack and cool completely before filling.

For Filling:

1. Combine all ingredients in a medium size bowl and beat until fluffy.
2. When cake is cool, unroll from towel and spread the cream cheese filling over the cake up to the edges.

3. Re-roll cake and wrap in plastic wrap. Refrigerate for at least 1 hour.

4. Dust with powdered sugar just before serving and slice crosswise into pieces.

Scooby Snacks

Ingredients:
- 1 stick butter

- 5 tablespoon granulated sugar

- 4 tablespoon brown sugar

- 1 egg

- A few drops of vanilla

- 1 cup flour

- 1 tablespoon cocoa powder

- 1/2 teaspoon baking soda

- 2/3 cup semisweet chocolate chips

- 1/2 cup chopped pecan s

- 1 ounce ground bud

Directions:
1. Preheat oven to 350 degrees F.
2. Grease three baking sheets.

3. Mix butter, sugars and weed in a bowl until fluffy. Beat the egg and vanilla in a separate bowl and add gradually to butter mixture.

4. Sift the flour, cocoa and baking soda over the mixture.

5. Add chocolate chips and nuts. Make small balls and space apart on baking sheet.

6. Bake for 15 minutes, then let cool.

Butterscotch Space Pops

Time Required: 40 minutes
Yield: 12 cannapops
Items Needed:
- Baking sheet

- Parchment paper

- Large saucepan

- Lollipop sticks

Ingredients:
- 1 cup sugar

- ½ cup cannabis corn syrup

- 2 tablespoons water

- 1 ½ teaspoons vinegar

- ¼ cup cannabutte r

- ¼ teaspoon vanilla extract

Directions:
1. Line baking sheet with waxed paper; set aside. Use cannabutter to grease the sides of the saucepan.
2. Combine the sugar, cannabis corn syrup, water and vinegar. Cook over medium-high heat for about 5 minutes, to boiling, stirring constantly with a wooden spoon to dissolve the sugar. Continue to cook the

mixture over medium heat, stirring constantly, while adding the butter (cut into 8 pieces), 2 pieces at a time.

3. The candy mixture should boil at a moderate, steady rate over the entire surface. Wait for the candy thermometer to read 300 degrees. This should take 25 to 30 minutes.

4. Remove the saucepan from the heat. Stir in the vanilla extract. Cool for 5 minutes. Pour the mixture, 1 to 2 tablespoons at a time, onto the lined baking sheets. The mixture will make 2 to 3 inch circles.

5. Quickly place a lollipop stick into each piece of candy, twisting gently to cover with the candy mixture. Let the lollipops harden. Wrap the lollipops individually in clear plastic wrap to store at room temperature.

Cannabis Monkey Bread

<u>Yield: 4-6 Servings</u>

If you've never had the privilege of eating monkey bread, look no further! The missing link to your happiness is here. Monkey bread is a fun, rip-apart bread, dripping in buttery and sugary goodness. This recipe is extremely simple to make, and generously feeds a good amount of people, making this a perfect breakfast dish.

Ingredients:
- 2 cans of original home-style pre-packaged biscuits (not the flaky-layers

- 1 cup sugar

- 2 oranges, zested

- 1 teaspoon cinnamon

- A pinch of sal t

- 1 cup light brown sugar

- 1 stick of butter

- 1 stick of cannabutter

- 1 tablespoon organic pure vanilla extract

Directions:

1. Preheat oven to 350 degrees F. Leave 2 cans of biscuits in the refrigerator until you plan on using them – the colder the biscuits, the less likely they will stick together during the sugar-coating process.

2. Add the white sugar, orange zest, cinnamon and a pinch of salt to a gallon-size, re-sealable plastic bag.

3. Once your sugar bag is ready, you may remove the two cans of biscuits from the refrigerator and open them. Using a pair of kitchen scissors, cut each biscuit into quarters. After cutting roughly 3-4 biscuits, add the pieces to the plastic bag, seal it, and shake the bag around until all the pieces are covered in the sugar/orange zest blend.

4. It is recommended that you add batches of 3 - 4 biscuits to the sugar bag at a time, as this will help prevent the pieces from clumping together into one big ball of dough. Repeat this process until both cans of biscuits are quartered, tossed in the sugar bag and evenly coated .

5. Generously spray your bundt pan with some non-stick baking spray, making sure to cover every nook and crevice.

6. Pour the contents of the bag evenly into your bundt pan, rearranging some pieces of biscuit, if need be. Set the bundt pan to the side for now.

7. In a medium skillet, heat your butter and cannabutter over medium to medium-low heat, until just about fully melted – do not burn the butter. Add in your light brown sugar and vanilla extract, and stir until almost thoroughly combined. It's okay if there are some small chunks of brown sugar still in the butter.

8. Then, carefully pour your butter/sugar mixture over the chunks of biscuit, turning the bundt pan as you pour to ensure even coverage. Shimmy the pan when you're done to make sure all the butter and sugar finds its way to the bottom of the pan.

9. Pop the bundt pan in the oven for 35-40 minutes, checking often towards the end of the cook time. No spaces in between bits of biscuit chunks should appear doughy, and the top of the monkey bread will have a delicious golden brown color.

10. Remove the bundt pan from the oven and onto a cooling rack for 10 minutes and WAIT! This is the most difficult part!

11. You need to allow the buttery, caramel sauce to cool enough so that when you flip over the bundt cake pan, the sauce does not drip all over and create a huge mess.

12. After 10 minutes, carefully flip and transfer your monkey bread to a large platter. Be careful as the bread will be extremely hot!

13. Serve and enjoy!

Coconut and Chocolate-Covered Marshmallow Cannabis Balls

Ingredients:
- 2 ounces butter
- 2 tablespoons cocoa
- 3 tablespoons condensed milk
- 2 ounce brown sugar
- 1/8 ounce finely ground hash or high-quality cannabis
- 6 ounces desiccated coconut
- 5 ounces small white marshmallows

Directions:
1. After melting the butter in a pan, mix in your cocoa, milk, sugar and hash. Continue to heat, stirring on occasion, until contents are melted together. Be very careful that you do not boil it.
2. Remove from the heat and add the majority of the coconut, saving just enough for a final coating. Now divide your mixture into 15 similarly size balls, and then flatten them just enough to be wrapped

around a marshmallow.

3. Once encasing a marshmallow, roll each of them in your remaining coconut until a generous coating has been applied.

4. We recommend only eating 1-2 per person, despite their tastiness.

Cannabis Cinnamon Roll Oatmeal Cookie

Ingredients:
- 10 packets cinnamon roll instant oatmea l
- 1 cup of firmly packed brown sugar
- 1 teaspoon baking soda
- 2 eggs
- 1 cup softened cannabutter
- 2 cups all-purpose flour
- 3/4 cup white sugar
- 1/4 cup of water

Directions:
1. Preheat your oven to 350 degrees F.
2. Mix butter and the sugars together until they're a creamy consistency.

3. Take the two eggs and beat them in. Then, add in both the flour and the baking soda, stirring continuously. Then, add in all of the oatmeal packets as well as the 1/4 cup of water.

4. Stir everything together until mixed evenly. The mixture should be like cookie dough.

5. Make small round balls out of the dough, and place on a greased cookie sheet.

6. Bake them in the oven for about 12 minutes, until they are golden brown. Remove the cookies from the sheet immediately, and put them on a plate to cool off before enjoying!